S0-ADC-297

A Year in Marrakesh

A YEAR IN MARRAKESH

PETER MAYNE

ELAND
LONDON

For M. H. M.

This edition published by Eland Publishing Limited
61 Exmouth Market, London EC1R 4QL in 2002

First published by John Murray
as *The Alleys of Marrakesh* in 1953
and by Eland in 1982

Text copyright © Peter Mayne 1953, 1982, 2002

ISBN 10: 0 907871 08 9
ISBN 13: 978 0 907871 08 8

All rights reserved. This publication may not be reproduced, stored in a retrieval system or transmitted in any form or by any means, electronic, mechanical, photocopying, recording or otherwise, without permission in writing from the publishers

Cover designed by Robert Dalrymple
Cover image shows a street scene in
Marrakesh (1937) © Sir Wilfred Thesiger
Permission granted by Curtis Brown Group Ltd/
Pitt Rivers Museum, University of Oxford
Drawings by Ronald Baillie
Map © Reginald Piggott

Text set in Great Britain by Antony Gray and
printed in Spain by GraphyCems, Navarra

Contents

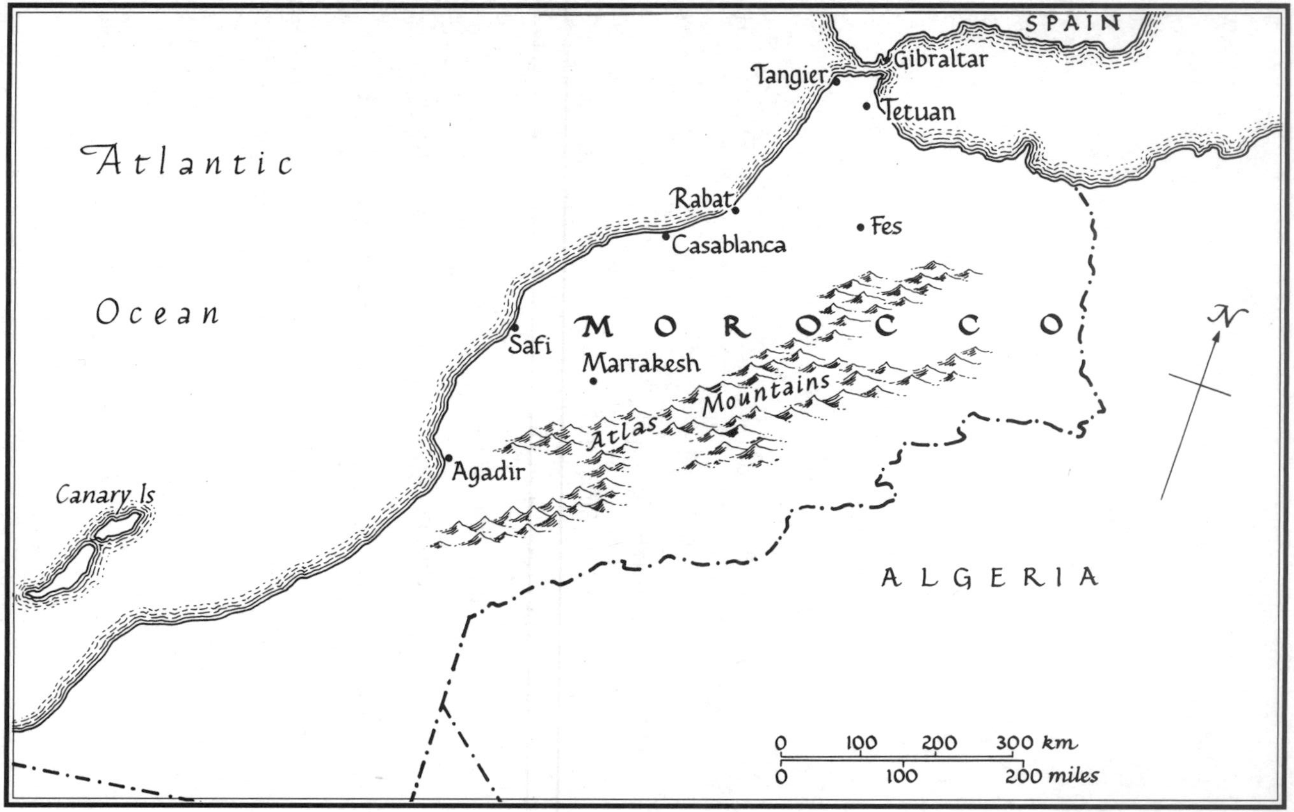
SPAIN
Gibraltar
Tangier
Tetuan
Atlantic
Ocean
Rabat
Casablanca
Fes
MOROCCO
Safi
Marrakesh
Atlas Mountains
Agadir
Canary Is
N
ALGERIA
0 100 200 300 km
0 100 200 miles

I

The Anteroom

I AM A STRANGER in these parts and Tangier feeds on the flesh of strangers. This is what they say, but no one has yet had so much as a bite out of me because I have sat myself behind carefully-chosen defences from which I shall slip unnoticed and be gone an hour from now.

At the table immediately in front of me are a big Spanish woman, three children and a man with blue-black hair. The children have been elaborately dressed for the occasion and are slapped when they fidget. 'Ignacio! Concepción! Tomás!' To left and right of me are other people at their tables – Spaniards, Moors, nondescripts – and every one of them is engrossed in the spectacle of the Sunday-evening *paseo*.

For better or worse, we are all gathered in the Socco Chico which is a *plaza* in the Moorish part of Tangier. Hundreds of us are immobilized thigh to thigh at café tables. Hundreds more are pressed still closer together on the little open *plaza* itself, where under the influence of some cosmic necessity they ebb and flow and sway, like algae in the shallows. Amongst them are creatures that dart about in the manner of fishes and smile with their teeth.

Anyway, here I am. My back is against the wall, or rather against a cast-iron grille which ventilates the interior of the café. There is a Cinzano on the table beside me and a siphon of aerated water. I am at a loss to know how ants have got into the siphon. Neither the ants themselves nor the people who filled the siphons can have intended this.

'Is it not rather warm,' people are asking themselves in their various languages, 'for the time of year?' It is spring and it *is* rather warm.

Sometimes a little breeze springs up and some of it is sucked into the café through the grille. At such moments the big Spanish woman tweaks at her corsage, and I think I feel cooler also. I have an hour in hand, my luggage is safely deposited at the terminus and I have escaped molestation hitherto, but I begin to fear that there is something behind that grille . . .

As I say, I am sitting in a little barricaded world of my own, here in the second row of café-terrace tables, and if the Tangier people suppose that I too am admiring them and their Sunday-evening walking-clothes, I would like to tell them that I am doing nothing of the sort. My eyes may be open, they may glint like little chips of coal, but it is not with desire. I have chosen to focus upon infinity, and for me infinity excludes Tangier and the present time and begins tomorrow at Latitude 31°40'. The Tangier people can look that up in their atlases, and they may sink or swim for all I care; they may send out distress signals or invitations to the valse, but they have no power to melt my heart or fascinate me. My eyes are open but unseeing. My ears are deaf, or nearly deaf . . . but if there really *is* someone behind that grille, then it is his voice that hums around the edges of my consciousness. I shall take no notice.

I am still sitting behind my defences, and there is now no doubt at all that an ill-wisher has discovered a chink in my back-plates through which he is repeatedly hissing a demand. He refuses to be ignored. He is saying –

' . . . *vous avez du feu, m'sieur, s'il vous plaît?*'

I passed a box of matches backwards over my shoulder without looking round. It was taken softly through the bars as it might be by a well-mannered parrot.

'*Merci, m'sieur. Tiens! ce sont des cigarettes anglaises que vous avez là?* You are English? If you wish I will try one. I am often glad to accept an English cigarette, *pour changer, n'est-ce pas*?'

I made no move. Someone put a handbill on to my table, leaning forward over the Spanish lady to do so. It said: HOY! HOY! TODAY! TONIGHT! LUCHA LIBRE. SO-AND-SO, THE BLACK MARVELLOUS! SO-AND-SO THE LOCAL SPLENDID! COME, COME, COME! My enemy must have paused to read it too.

After a brief interval the voice said, 'Ah. All-In Wrestle.' It paused again. Then, 'Sir. I have something to say, something you will wish to know.' There was another pause and he repeated the last sentence.

I did not look round. Instead I said clearly in French, because it seemed more impersonal, 'There is nothing that one wishes to know.'

'I have been watching. Guarding over you, sir, from the *intérieur*. I have seen all! That girl, for example – the girl in the *costume aux paillettes*. Sir! I implore you!'

I said, 'Leave me in peace.'

'You do not know! You are strange to Tangier. *I* know. I have seen the regards exchanged, the balancing of the haunch. Sir, that girl will destroy you in a twink!'

I pretended to have heard nothing.

'Sir, look at me! Turn and look! You will find that I am a nobleman of Morocco. I love your country England and, as my brothers, I love your countrymen English whose language I have learned so fluent from a Swedish gentleman now dead (rest in peace). You risk to suffer because of your strangeness. This I *will* not see. If you should be heated, then let me advise and assist.'

Had the Swedish gentleman really spoken English like this? I turned slowly and looked at the speaker. He was about twenty-five, brownish and shabby. It was not a bad face – round, with big, black, startled eyes, and when he saw me looking at him he smiled socially and said: 'Let me present myself. I am Moulay Hamed – or, as you would say, the Seigneur Hamed. I have the *entrée* into all the houses because of my nobleness. You will kindly tell me your name and business and permit me to lead you to some private place where each of the girls is beautiful – and blood-tested by physicians. By *diploma'd* physicians.'

The language and the prospect were equally fascinating but I said coldly, 'If you do not leave me, I shall leave you.'

'But we have only just met!'

'The meeting will do no good to either of us.'

'Listen! You are strange here . . . '

'I am not in the least strange anywhere. I was quite happy till you came to pester me.'

I had turned round on him again and spoke with an indignation that must have shocked him. He seemed crestfallen. He was obviously a very unsuccessful guide. You had only to look at the others with their flashing self-confidence to know that this poor creature was a failure. I even felt sorry for him.

He then said, 'Please remain seated. I come to sit at your table.'

'Now *you* listen,' I replied firmly. 'I am a mad person who does not think it strange to be alone and to know nothing, and within a few minutes I shall be gone from here, and I am praying that where I am going I shall find a world where guides are born with the mark on them, so that – '

'Going? Where? Oh, sir, *where?*' he broke in.

' – so that they can be identified by their mamas and strangled before – '

'But *where* are you going, sir?' he broke in again, excitedly.

'I am going to Marrakesh. By the night train.'

'*Insha'Allah,*' he breathed. Then his face widened into an ecstatic smile. 'What! To Marrakesh, you say? Sir, I have a cousin in Marrakesh, equally noble as me, with whom it is possible to lodge for he is *propriétaire* of hotel! *Very* select. Look! I have a photograph of my cousin dressed in Arabic with his friend before the *Bureau de Poste* of the Place Djema'a el-Fna at Marrakesh. You wish to see?'

And suddenly I found myself with his wallet in my hand and Seigneur Hamed no longer behind the grille. I knew then that I had been mistaken, that the Seigneur was after all at the top of his profession.

* * *

Is it a strength or a weakness, not to know when you are beaten? I did not know yet. Instead I temporized. An Arab hotel? It would be an appropriate start. I told myself that I needed just the sort of help in Marrakesh that the

Seigneur or his cousin could provide. I saw no point in going there to live the life of a European tourist. I also told myself that I was perfectly capable of defending myself and that the boredom – the ineffable boredom! – of half an hour with the Seigneur could be turned to account. I allowed him to join me at my table and the first few minutes were spent explaining why I would not take him with me to Marrakesh. I said that this was not just an excursion but – but he could not understand the distinction I was trying to make. How then could I hope he would understand the whole truth, that I was on the eve of a personal rebirth at which his presence could serve no purpose? So I didn't speak of this. I merely said that I had barely enough money to support myself, let alone to fill two stomachs. While these facts were taking root in his mind, I allowed him to show me the contents of his little plastic *portefeuille*. First, the photograph of the cousin. I was asked to admit that his cousin was handsome and I said yes willingly enough, though the photograph showed nothing so positive. Most of the picture was taken up by a decorative mount – camels, palm trees, a representation of the famous Koutoubia minaret and other emblems of the south. There was not much room for the two little heads, one in a tarboosh, the other in a skullcap and both so sadly blurred. Nevertheless I admired both the young men. Then I admired photographs of the Seigneur himself.

'You consider good?' he asked doubtfully. '*I* consider that I am made to appear less well than real. The photographer is not good. Next time,' he added, putting the pictures reluctantly aside, 'I shall make my portraits at the best – the studio Foto Venus.'

He took up his identification papers. Then some postcards of Nice and Cap Ferrat that he had received from grateful clients. We read the messages together. Next, behind talc, pictures of Egyptian film stars, pin-up girls of which a brief, exciting glimpse would be obtained each time the *portefeuille* was opened. And finally, as I was handing back a surprisingly complimentary Police Certificate of *Bonne Vie et Moeurs* that he had spread out for me to read, I said as lightly as possible, 'Perhaps I shall see your cousin and give him news of you.'

This, as I had hoped, started a train of thought which appealed to the

Seigneur. As lightly as I had spoken he replied, 'What if I give my cousin a letter . . . ?' The suggestion took shape: he would write a letter to his cousin and I would carry it to Marrakesh. This letter would cause all doors to fly open before me. Leaving his *portefeuille* as a guarantee that I would remain at the table, he darted across the Socco Chico to a *tabac* and returned with a piece of paper and an envelope.

'The pen, please,' he said.

It cost him an effort, but in due course a letter was written in Arabic, and signed. The signature was in Roman characters, to impress. He was on the point of licking down the flap when he paused, took up his *portefeuille* again and routed about in it.

He did not find what he was searching for, so he turned to me and said quite casually, 'I was intending to put a thousand-franc note into the letter. I wish to send this little sum to my cousin by your hand so that he may respect you and accord you favours.'

'Thank you,' I said non-committally.

We both knew that there was no money in the *portefeuille*.

'*Eh bien, que voulez-vous?* I find I have left my money in my house.' He sighed and looked out into the *place*. It was as full as ever. Two sombre-looking men were whispering together and throwing covert glances in our direction. The girl in the *costume aux paillettes* had disappeared but there were many others, some with eyes downcast demurely, others less demure. Seigneur Hamed was taking a deep breath: 'Never mind. To-morrow you shall come to my house and I shall offer a banquet of *couscous*. You know *couscous*? You have tasted it already? Delicious. And then I shall put the money in the letter.'

'I am leaving now. By the night train.'

He knew this too, but he allowed the information to shock him.

'Then, my dear friend, there is nothing that can be done. It is too late. *O malheur!* You, who beg me to arrange *logement* with my cousin who has the hotel, a true Arab hotel in Marrakesh. Alas, you will be obliged to lodge in a common European hotel like any common European tourist. What a sad thing!' He took up the siphon, shook it briskly to work up the pressure and aimed a preliminary squirt on to the floor. I think this must have been to skim off the ants. Then he seemed to notice that his glass was already empty of Cinzano again and looked at me inquiringly. I did not offer him another. Instead I said, 'You owe your cousin money?'

'Owe? I told you I wished to *give* him fifteen hundred francs and that if you care to carry the money to him he will certainly . . . '

'You said a thousand.'

'I mentioned I was sending a thousand *now* in the letter, and the rest is to follow, of course.'

I said nothing for a moment and then murmured, 'I was thinking of giving you a small reward for your kindness in offering me an introduction to your cousin. If you like I will pay him some money as if it were from you. Shall I do that?' I fished out a five hundred-franc note from my pocket to show the extent of my generosity.

He pondered for a moment in his turn. 'Perhaps . . . Yes. If you give him five hundred francs, then *this* . . . ' He did not even name the sum as he took hold of one corner of the note I still held firmly. 'This I will keep till I receive my cousin's assurance that he has carried out my wishes about your comfort and happiness. That is my principal concern, and then only will I send the *second* five hundred to him. That is best, I am sure; and businesslike. And the *third* five hundred note you may deposit also with me and . . . '

'It is for me to decide the amount,' I said. 'I will give him five hundred francs only.'

'*Bon*. Very well, just as I said, you will pass five hundred francs to my cousin with the letter and I will hold the second and the third five hundred francs and send to him only when – '

'*I* am making the rules.'

We glared at each other. I started again. 'Look!' I said, adroitly flicking the note out of his grasp and at the same time taking some notes of smaller denomination from my pocket. 'Look! Here are five one-hundred franc notes. *Three*, I will hand to your cousin with your letter. *Two*, I will leave with you. They are yours, these two hundred francs. You can keep them, or send them to your cousin, as you please.'

'If God wills,' he said softly. '*Insha' Allah*. You know that we Arabs always say this? "If God wills." It is necessary to say it.' He continued rather sourly, 'But the sum of which you speak comes to only five hundred francs if I mistake not. Your *calcul* is at fault, sir. *We* are speaking of fifteen hundred francs.'

'The sum of which I am speaking is the sum I consider your services are worth to me. I have made a very careful *calcul*, taking account of the Cinzano you have consumed at my expense, your commission from the *patron* of the café, and I have added a little extra payment against your various other services offered but declined.'

'If that is your *calcul*, sir, I cannot be sure that you will be well received by my cousin. I have already written "one thousand" in the letter.'

'But now you know the truth.'

'*Now*, of course, on reading the letter my cousin will tell himself and the other important personages of Marrakesh that you have retained most of the money I have given you to give to him. Sir, I do not think that you will be well received.'

'The letter can be changed.'

'The doors will not open,' he said smugly, ignoring me.

'The letter can be changed.'

'*Kifash?* Mm–m . . . It can be changed if I change it.' He was looking mistily at a plump little girl, waving his hand to her in a lordly manner to which she did not, however, respond.

'Then change it,' I said. He did not pay any attention as I flicked the notes in his face. 'You agree or not?'

'Very well,' he said at last. 'I agree. But only because we are firm friends. If we were not firm friends I could never agree to so unjust – '

'Take the pen and write. Write *five* hundred francs. Write it in figures. That is the sum I will hand to your cousin.'

'My cousin is unable to read French figures.'

'It is not for your cousin that you must write it; it is for *me*.'

He swung round, affronted. 'You do not trust me?'

'No,' I said.

'How then can I trust you with all this money? Tell me that, sir!'

I let him sit there with his eyes blazing for a few seconds. Then I said,

'I do not ask you to trust me. It is I who have to trust you. Moreover, I have decided to give you two hundred and fifty francs for yourself. Now write!'

He compressed his lips and then opened them with the noise of a little bubble bursting. 'You have tricked me. You are hard like stone. But a noble does not go back upon his word. Give me the pen!'

*   *   *

It is rather a peculiar arrangement. Actually, it is the first Moroccan bargain I have ever struck and it is proper that I should pay too much to begin with.

2

Derb el-Bir

I JUST STEPPED OUT of the train and allowed myself to be carried on the bosom of the crowd that was already milling towards the exit. In this manner I arrived into my new world this morning: no pain, no cutting of the umbilical cord, no cries – except those of the weaklings who went under in the flood, and I had no thought for them. I could see the sun shining at the end of the *sortie* passage. I supposed that the porter had my luggage and I certainly had my ticket somewhere, but no one had time to ask for it as the flood burst through the final barriers. I stood there exultant in the station yard, and all about me *djellabas*, veiled women, babies who could fill their lungs and scream now that the ordeal was over. I was silent and alone in the knowledge that this was the very moment of rebirth.

'. . . *ssss–Americán–*you!' It was my porter, flushed and triumphant, '*Tu veux calèche?*'

He was choosing from a row of ancient victorias and I didn't trouble to tell him that I was English.

'This one,' he said. An enormous coal-black coachman was taking charge of me. I confess I thought his horse looked less solid than its driver, but my suitcase and typewriter were already on the box, and they were almost lifting me on to the red leather upholstery at the back.

'*Toi Americán?*' the coachman asked, pointing at me. I was busy paying off the porter – the regulation fee was marked on his brassard.

'*Je suis anglais*,' I said.

The porter stopped protesting at my meanness and looked disappointed. '*Americán est gentil*,' he commented.

'I also am *gentil*, but poor.'

'Ah–h . . .'

I followed up my advantage. 'You are poor too, aren't you?' I asked them, and they said yes, they were. 'Well, *I* think that poor is more *gentil* than rich.'

They nodded and agreed about this and the porter asked for a cigarette, so I handed him my pack from which he took two, one for himself and the second for the coachman. There was one left for me. We lit cigarettes for each other ceremoniously. When this had been done, the porter graciously accepted his fee.

'Remember,' he said, indicating his brassard. '*Numéro six*. Me. Unnerstan?' He caught hold of my hand and shook it.

The coachman was asking, '*Où tu vas?*' I now had time to look at him properly: very large, night-blue, a shirt, pantaloons fastened below the knee and a floppy straw hat. I handed over the Seigneur's letter.

'It is written on this,' I said.

The coachman took the letter and climbed on to his box, but starting took a little while. He had first to get his whip warmed up, describing leather arabesques in the air with it before he suddenly flicked his wrist and the thong cracked like a pistol-shot. After this frightening preliminary of which the horse took no notice at all, he thickened his throat and released a strangled '*. . . eeee–yuh!*' We creaked forward into motion. The porter was waving from the pavement. '*A tout-à-l'heure!*' he called after us.

This, I thought to myself, looking round at the half-built French town, is still only the anteroom. Somewhere over there is the true city of Marrakesh, though I can't see it yet.

Quite some way over there, too, as far as I could judge from the Tariff of Fares beside me. A journey within the new French town, I read, would cost a certain sum; a journey over the boundaries of time into the old Moorish city, so much – a great deal more; *Le Tour des Remparts*, a very considerable sum. Were the ramparts as long as all that? Would they be visible soon?

The road was blue with fallen jacaranda blossom, the air yellow with sunshine.

* * *

The French have a passion for *ronds-points* from which identical avenues radiate like the points of stars. How neat it is, but how confusing! In spite of the turning wheels and the stumbling of the horse's hooves, there was no sense of movement. Even the scenery remained stationary: the avenue, ourselves forever beneath the same jacaranda, the same villa to the left of us, the same vacant plot to the right. Everything so new. Were all these objects moving with us under the vertical sun? Were *we* moving? And then suddenly we were again at a *rond-point* – not the same one, surely – not again and again! A ninety-degree section of the landscape had started to wheel about us, flat and improbable, little half-grown trees and half-built villas, signposts pointing hither and thither and bearing the names of Generals, Presidents of the Republic and such, and we were still where we had always been.

We had been going for some while when the coachman reined in his horse. He turned on his box, pushing back his straw hat so that he could look at me. I could now see that he wore a little brown crocheted skullcap under the straw hat, and that the two together formed a sort of ball-and-socket joint, enabling him to set his straw hat at a very daring angle without losing it. He smiled down and asked: '*Où, tu dis?*'

Where, indeed! Alas, neither the coachman nor I could read the address on Seigneur Hamed's envelope, he because he could not read at all and I because I can only read in Arabic the words I already know, and then only if I have written them myself – and I had not written these.

'*Shī bās mā kāin,*' he said comfortingly. 'Never mind.'

We continued our journey. There was a Moor sleeping under the jacaranda tree now and we asked him to help. He could not read either. Someone else was walking vaguely in the same direction as ourselves so he got in and clop-clopped with us for a bit, clutching at the letter or my hand or by some other means demonstrating his concern – but he could not read, he said. Another just waggled his hands helplessly from the side of the road when the coachman shouted to him. They were all torn with anxiety to know where I was going. For myself, I was content to sit back against the red leather and let these kind people solve my problem. In the end it was solved, of course. Another victoria was approaching from the opposite direction; we hailed it and in a minute we were alongside in mid-road, stationary. An elderly Moor was in the back of the other. 'He is *fkih*,' my coachman said complacently. I didn't know what he meant exactly, but evidently amongst other things it meant that the old Moor would be able to read the address for us, and this proved to be the case. I think my coachman must have asked the *fkih* to open the letter and read the contents too, because the old man nodded and produced a long, rusty wire. But I whisked the letter away before he could get the wire under the flap. I saw no reason why they should read it, harmless though it was. They looked surprised. It was then suggested that I pay the old man a small fee and I did so, but I believe the other coachman pocketed it. We bowed from our victorias, whips cracked, '*eeee–yuh*', and the others drew away.

'Derb el-Bir,' my coachman said. 'Moulay Ibrahim. Why did you not say?'

At last we knew where we were going, but before we did anything else, the coachman wanted to erect the hood – to shield the fine red leather. It was well after one o'clock and he felt that the sun threatened it. He had not thought of this before, he said, but now he remembered too that I had no hat. I didn't want the hood because it would impede my view – my first view of Marrakesh. We tried to explain our differing viewpoints and the coachman appealed to a passer-by who ruled after some thought that, whereas the sun would go down later in the day, Marrakesh would remain in place, if God willed it so, and that I would then have my first view of the city when the sun had lost its power to spoil red leather and unprotected heads. I wanted to see *now*, and said so again.

'You have seen *now*,' the coachman said patiently. 'Only little trees. Look!'

The hood was lowered like a vast black cowl round me. By bending forward over my knees and looking up sideways I could still have obtained the first symbolic glimpse of my new life as soon as it came into view, but I chose instead to lean back against the upholstery, sullenly seeing nothing. I was aware, nevertheless, of a towering red wall that had edged in beside us after a while, and then of the coachman's voice calling to me, '*Regarde!* Koutoubia! *Mezīn!*' I declined to look. Then I realized that we were leaving the trim French avenues and had reached a waste land, treeless, without shadow. A donkey passed in the opposite direction, very perky on the points of its hooves. We overtook a group of square-toed shoes and some bare feet. A truck whirled by in a flurry and in front of us a truss of bamboos trailed their disconsolate feathers along the road. The bamboos were supported at the far end, as I discovered in a moment, by a man so small that I could see as high as his beard. Then, without warning, deep shadows closed round us and we were under what must be a city gate, cut through walls as thick as a house, red and crumbling with age. We turned sharply to the right, then to the left again and out into a subaqueous light flickering with dust particles. The victoria was surrounded by feet and voices, *djellaba*-hems, the wheels of bicycles, by the tumult of a city and of streets too narrow for the life that had crammed itself into them. Still I refused to look out. I had come this far with my nose to the ground; I would complete the journey this way. Most of the noises that pressed in on me seemed less words than sounds – warnings, encouragements, snatches of song. The victoria was coming to a stop.

Without a word, the coachman clambered down and left me. His feet went striding down a side alley and out of my restricted line of vision. I sat waiting. Some children came and poked their heads in under the hood to stare at me. They varied from black to brownish. I stared back at them but grew bored with staring. We did not speak. They went away after a while. No one seemed in the least concerned that our victoria was blocking two-thirds of the roadway, and this unconcern was justified by the fact that nothing came down the street that was too large to edge past us. Within a few minutes I saw the coachman's feet again, accompanied this time by a strange pair, visible under a *djellaba*. The two men came up to the victoria and looked in. I was being shown to the newcomer – a plump youth – and they resumed their chatter, too fast for me to follow it. The youth was reading Seigneur Hamed's letter again. He introduced himself: Si 'Abdelqadir. I was invited to get out of the victoria and a thin, consumptive-looking creature came forward to collect the baggage. Together, the five of us – for the coachman came too – we started down the alley.

This was my first interior view of Marrakesh, and it told me nothing. A mean back street, blank walls on either side, a street sign, DERB EL-BIR in Roman and Arabic characters. The monotony of plastered masonry was broken only by a door within a door, a dozen yards ahead, heavy and studded with metal.

'*Par ici*,' the youth said as we reached the door. I was relieved to find that he spoke French. There was no signboard to indicate that it was a hotel.

Everything was settled very amicably. There was of course a formal and noisy dispute over the sum owing to the coachman, during which I quoted the printed fare tariff and he pooh-poohed it. Then another over the meaning of Seigneur Hamed's letter, and finally the cousin was called. He was obviously someone quite other than the larger of the two young men in the photograph taken outside the *Bureau de Poste* of the Place Djema'a el-Fna. In fact, he wasn't young at all but approaching middle age, with a heavy face framed in beard. He could speak no French and of course I could not yet trust my Arabic, so the friend acted as interpreter. I was told the cousin's name: Moulay Ibrahim. 'What did I say?' the coachman commented. Then I was asked to say exactly how much money had been sent by my hand. I told them. How long, then, did I wish to stay? And when would I pay the balance of the sum owing? It was not at all usual to take lodgers – European lodgers, they amended quickly; and another lengthy dispute followed in which I tried to get it into their heads that, though I was in no way responsible for Seigneur Hamed's debts, hope would not die so long as I was accommodated in comfort and happiness. They exchanged glances. When I asked the cost of the lodging, they were suddenly calm and sweet.

'*Si peu, si peu*,' the youth 'Abdelqadir said. 'Nothing. Nearly nothing.

'*Shī bās mā kāin* – there is no harm in it. *Yallah!*'– and he led the way up a staircase from the little vestibule to my room. Moulay Ibrahim followed, breathing heavily.

Halfway up, Moulay Ibrahim called something to 'Abdelqadir who looked back and nodded, and I had an impression of collusion. Why not? Were they not in a sense banded against me, as well as under some sort of polite obligation?

'Enter!' 'Abdelqadir said, as he threw open a small door to let me pass in before him.

The room was like a little luminous box: long and narrow, white plaster walls – though not very white – white plaster ceiling with open beams also plastered. I walked across to the window and glanced out. There was a patio below with rooms all round it. Then I turned back into the room intending to say how nice it was – indeed it was a great deal better than I had expected – and caught the youth fussing about behind the door. Moulay Ibrahim made a startled little noise in his throat; the youth whisked something out of sight behind his back. Something fell to the floor with a tiny clatter in the silence. It was a drawing-pin. I stooped to pick it up and caught sight of a stiffish white card that 'Abdelqadir was trying unsuccessfully to stuff into the side pocket of his *djellaba*.

'What's that?' I asked him.

But it was only the notice registered hotels are bound to display in each room; the notice showing the room number and the authorized rate per diem, together with certain rules of the establishment. I took it from him. Room No. 8. The price was Fr. 155.00 per diem, plus 'service' 10 per cent.

'*Rakhīs*,' Moulay Ibrahim muttered sadly. 'Cheap . . . '

It was certainly cheap. I wondered what they had intended to charge me.

* * *

It was a small room. Its narrow wall just contained a bedstead – brass. It jangled when I thumped it to test the mattress. There was nothing else in the way of furniture except a sort of collapsible table, a stool and an old, leather-covered chest. I don't pretend that there was any practical advantage in transferring my clothes from my suitcase to the chest, but it was a symbol that the journey was over, and so I unpacked. Then I hid my suitcase under the bed. I hate to see luggage lying about. It means journeys. Dogs often feel the same way and get nervous of luggage.

I could lay my palm flat on the ceiling. If I stood by the window overlooking the patio, my shoulders overtopped it comfortably. The window was deeply recessed in the thickness of the wall and the obvious place to sit, so I fetched the pillow from the bed and used it for a cushion. How thick the wall was: two foot, at least. The plaster was badly chipped here and there, and the masonry showed through. I think it was just plain Marrakesh earth, pounded hard and then faced. No wonder they build so thick, if this is the case.

The sun came streaming through the grille, casting its 'S' patterns over me and the shiny surface of the floor. I sat there, looking down into the patio where I could see the patron and his friend at a draughtboard. The opposing teams were Coca-Cola and Pepsi-Cola bottle-tops. The patron would remain silent for a minute and then suddenly slap a bottle-top into its new position. Then he would swing back in triumph, but his friend, 'Abdelqadir, affected to be unmoved. It occurred to me that I had had nothing all day except *petit déjeuner* on the platform at Casablanca while waiting for the Marrakesh connection; not even anything to drink. I called out to the patron and his friend from the window: '*Du thé à la menthe, s'il vous plaît. Est-ce possible? Ici? Dans la chambre?*'

'*Wāhād ātay!*' the patron shouted, without looking up. '*Nīmero tmenya!*' The porter appeared for a moment, nodded and then went into the vestibule. *Nīmero tmenya.* I notice that when Moors make use of French words, the French 'u' sharpens still further and becomes 'ī'. *Nīmero.*

'*Merci!*' I called down to them.

It was after half-past two. I wanted my mint tea and the long wait exasperated me. It seemed such a waste of time, when Marrakesh was waiting outside, so I went to the top of the stairs and shouted down to the porter. Nobody answered. I turned back into my room. There was a little ladder clamped to the wall beside the door that I had not noticed when I arrived. It led up to a broken wooden trap, flush with the ceiling. The roof, obviously. I climbed it and pushed the trap open.

For some time I stood there on the roof, looking slowly about me. I felt a little *exalté* and yet deflated. Arrival is such a definite thing; it is hard to live up to it. Yet this was what I had chosen, out of all the possibilities in the world. It was in order to be here and nowhere else that I had laid my plans, solemnly, as if it mattered profoundly, with neither knowledge nor experience to guide me. It was, of course, profoundly important to me, but in a manner that I had altogether failed to explain to anyone else. I don't think I had really expected my friends to understand. If you are determined to do something irrational, it is best not to tell your friends, but I had tried to tell some, and they had been happy to explain how stupid I was. I had even shown my air ticket to one.

'Ah,' he said, nodding wisely. 'A return ticket. I see it's valid for six months. I wish *I* could get away for a six-month holiday.' And he looked at me like people look at children they are ready to humour a little.

'I'm going there indefinitely,' I said. 'The return half is just in case . . . I can always sell it back.'

'Oh, I see. I think you ought to have the courage of your convictions, Peter, however peculiar. Why Marrakesh, I wonder . . . though it's attractive, I hear; smart, too. Isn't there a magnificent hotel that Mr Churchill goes to? The Mamounia, or something?'

'I believe there is.'

Then he looked pensive, and a little triumphant perhaps, 'Lucky to be able to afford it.'

He knew perfectly well that I could not, but I didn't choose to think about it and, standing there on the roof, my first impressions were filled with hope.

The world was sharp under the sunlight. In Tangier they had told me that I was mad to come here so late in the season. 'It will be a furnace,' people said. But it wasn't. Not yet, in any case. The air was soft and limpid. The plain of Marrakesh lay flat into the distance and beyond it the horseshoe of the High Atlas, snow still lying on the peaks. Everything was brilliantly defined – the mountains, the plain, the immense palm groves beyond the city walls, the city itself, gardens within the city, flat roofs round me in a complex of horizontal planes pierced with minarets. I could see the Koutoubia so high and beautiful over this flat city, and there was another minaret almost as beautiful. The panorama was full of these pointing fingers, but the only one I could identify was the Koutoubia. There were cypresses and Japanese lilac marking the larger patios. All this crowding detail, lit with the clarity of a *trompe-l'oeil*! I deliberately emptied my mind and stood there, not even looking, but warm with delight.

The noise of the city droned in my ears, somnolent afternoon noises mostly, but from somewhere there came a roaring, diffused with distance, like a great many people far away; their voices merged into one voice, the sea heard in a seashell.

I looked down on to our patio and then wandered across to the other side of the roof. I was above an alley bustling with life. It was clearly not the alley by which I had been brought here. An old beggar-woman was squatting below me and I tried to drop a coin into her hand. The coin went rolling away under the wheels of a bicycle, but someone ran after it and picked it up for the beggar. The man on the bicycle fell off as a result, and people crowded round to see what had been broken. But nothing was broken. The man who had collected the coin was telling the beggar-woman that it had dropped from above. He was shouting into her ear and pointing upwards, but she just nodded patiently as if that was what she would expect. She didn't even trouble to look up. Then suddenly a woman in a violent headscarf started screaming at me from a neighbouring roof. She was unveiled and carried an armful of washing. Her screams affronted me. I was for a moment transported back to another Muslim city, Peshawar, I would have known what to shout back if I had still been living in Peshawar, where women aren't allowed to scream at strangers. But here I was tongue-tied and helpless, and angry too. From below in our patio the patron's friend was screaming at me as well. He had risen from the draughtboard.

'*Descends! Descends toi!*'

I descended. I had forgotten already, though I had read of this somewhere. Rooftops are sacred to the womenfolk in Morocco. In theory, these poor encloistered creatures live out their lives in their homes, only coming up for air to the roof to peg out the washing, squatting by the parapet to natter to the neighbours' women, exchanging gossip. Once a week, twice perhaps, they will make a furtive veiled sortie to the *hammām*, passing quickly through the wicked alleyways, attended by slaves carrying soap, towels and unguents. This is the theory, based on what is considered proper to the wives of the rich, but the writer of what I had been reading said it was extended to include all women as a sex. I don't care to break rules till I know how to do so with impunity, so I descended.

The tea hadn't come, but it came in the end. It was already cold when it arrived, so perhaps the porter – *gardien*, I should call him – had had to fetch it from a café; perhaps there was no café nearby. I no longer wanted it, but I drank it and I remember deciding that tepid mint tea is nastier than hot. I already knew, from experience in Tangier, that hot mint tea is to be preferred to Moorish coffee. The glass was cracked so that the sticky, sugary liquid seeped through on to my fingers and there was no wash-basin in the room. Nevertheless, there was a tap sticking jauntily out from the wall near the door. When it came to the point, no water flowed from it.

I went down to make a formal complaint, passing the *gardien* on my way through the vestibule. He did not look up. But when I reached the patio, the patron listened to my complaint and made a formal apology through the intermediary of his French-speaking friend. He added his own little gesture of resignation when he saw that the youth had come to the part about '. . . *ti vois, monsieur, ça marche pas.*' 'We poor mortals . . . ' murmured the patron's hands, waving disconsolately. Then the youth very kindly got up from the draughts game, took me by the fingers and led me back to the vestibule. '*Voilà!*' he cried, pointing. There was a tap near the *gardien*. I could take a bucket, the youth said, fill it and carry it back into the patio and wash myself beside the lavatory door.

'The face, the hands, the feet,' he went on, indicating each member in turn, 'For that . . . ' and he now indicated the rest of the body, 'the *hammām*.'

It seemed reasonable enough, if you had no bathroom. There would be no difficulty about the *hammām*, I was told, even though Christians were not normally admitted, because the *gardien* would be happy to arrange everything.

The *gardien* did not look inclined to arrange anything at all.

* * *

I had no fixed plan when I left the hotel – except that I wanted to see Marrakesh, or something of it, while the daylight still held – so I wandered slowly through the little covered market near our alleyway. Bazaar, *souq*, it's the same thing in essence, tiny shops, *épiciers*, barbers, a *tabac* in which the packets of cigarettes were arranged in a square frame balanced on one point and divided into compartments for the different brands. I have never smoked 'black' tobacco with any pleasure, but it's time to start now, so I resisted 'Gold Flake' and chose 'Casa Sport', black as night, fifty francs for twenty. A *calèche* was standing nearby with a passenger in it, the driver calling out lackadaisically, 'Djema'a el-Fna! Djema'a el-Fna!' Seeing me there, uncertainly in front of the *tabac*, he called to me: '*Ssss!* M'soo! Djema'a el-Fna? *Tu viens? Monte!*'

The Moor in the back moved into a corner of the seat to make room. Djema'a el-Fna? Yes. It was one of the things to see. The guidebooks give it a paragraph: it is a big *place*, noisy, crowded. 'Animated,' they say, 'a perpetual fairground where men of the Sahara rub shoulders with the more gentle folk of the Sus . . . ' Sus? A valley beyond the Atlas, I think. I got in.

'Do you mind?' I asked the other man, hoping he would know French. He did, sufficiently.

'*Monte,*' he said. I suppose this is the custom and that the fare is apportioned between the passengers.

We talked a little. He wanted to know who I was and what was my nationality, and when he heard that I was to stay at Moulay Ibrahim's hotel, he said '*Tiens!*' and seemed pleased. 'Moulay Ibrahim is my *camarade*,' he said. '*Gentil.*'

'Derb el-Bir. Does it mean something?'

'*Oui*. Road of the Well.'

'Is there one?'

'*Peut-être.*'

I asked his name and he told me, adding that he was from Rehamna. A district, perhaps, or a town, I didn't know, but he seemed to think it important. He knew a great many people and was frequently obliged to bow in response to greetings.

'*Ecoute!*' He was leaning forward, listening. 'You hear? Djema'a el-Fna. You have seen before?'

'No. I only arrived today.'

It was the roaring I had heard from our roof, but nearer now, and when finally we came to the source of it, it was a frenzy of sound.

The Djema'a el-Fna covers a wide area – perhaps fifteen hundred square yards or more, irregularly shaped. A road follows one side of it and there is nothing to separate the *place* from the road except a slight depression for drainage. They say it has existed as long as the Koutoubia which looks down on it from the end of a vista – and that means the twelfth century. But it has been asphalted since those days. They also say that it is never empty, and it could certainly never be more crowded than it was when I came upon it that evening before sunset. A huge wide crowded *place*, but something more than that too. It has a strange quality and when you look closer you find that the sky seems to sail above it as if the two were part of the same cosmic plan. It has something of the sea, an inland, tideless sea, waves of *djellaba*-hoods, a flecking of skullcaps, moving closely together, so close that identities merge into the general turbulence. Standing on the brink, you can follow the course of the currents with your eyes; the slow, apparently aimless movement of them and then a whirlpool which seems to stand still at the rim with its spinning centre empty except for a dancer, or a man spinning a matchlock so fast that it has flattened out into a metal saucer. And then, without warning, the whirlpool disintegrates and dies, leaving the mass to flow forward into the emptiness, filling the void.

For some minutes I felt a strange elation, but when I went nearer I found myself cut off from it. I wandered through the crowds, peeping over shoulders into the whirlpools, seeing nothing any more but the faces and whatever they happened to be watching. It was simply a fairground again: singers, an ostrich standing among the bones of its fellows, a woman who drinks boiling water from a kettle to the accompaniment of flutes. Boys – *Chleuhs*, someone told me – like little white mice pirouetting and squeaking and clinking their minute finger-cymbals. Charlatans of all sorts. It is a long list. In the old days there were other things for the people to look at, the guidebook says – decapitated heads, specifically. It gives a translation of the name, Djema'a el-Fna: Congregation of the Departed. With the coming of the French Protectorate, the decapitations were stopped, but the people still crowd the *place* just the same, and I shall come too. There is something living here which I would like to share, a sort of animal force that we have forgotten about in the temperate zones.

The people seem to have three kinds of face – a long, a square, and a round, the colour varying from a black that is almost blue to a pink that could well be European. They are good-tempered and polite, but they took no notice of me – and why should I expect them to? I am as outlandish to them as they are to me, and if I want to make contact with them, it is I who must move first.

* * *

I have been in Marrakesh several days now.

It is easy enough to find the Café de France, even without a guide. It is the grandest of all the cafés in the medina, and one of three that give on to the Djema'a el-Fna – one of four, if you count a fourth that has only a sideways, corner-of the eye view. Moreover, if you sit on the road-level terrace of the Café de France and are content with a *café simple*, it is no more expensive than any other café, and this means that anyone in the position to buy himself a coffee anywhere can use it. Professional guides are said to use it too, as a sort of club, but the season for tourists is over for this year.

The roof of the café is particularly smart. On the roof *consommation* is *obligatoire*, so you can't just sit there and buy nothing. If you want a coffee on the roof, moreover, it has to be a *filtre* at nearly twice the cost of a road-level *café simple*. All drinks cost more there, but of course you do have the view and you can see the people milling about in the *place* below, the ostrich and the tumblers, the fire-eaters, the *charmeurs-de-serpents* and nearly three hundred degrees of Marrakeshi rooftops against the background of the Atlas.

Yes. The roof is certainly very smart, yet it has this disadvantage: no one who is not on the roof also can see you being smart there, and that – for some – makes the surcharges less worth paying. Guides take their clients up during the tourist season, but that is a different thing again: guides are there in the way of business, to point out the Pasha's palace and the silhouette of the Hotel Mamounia, which much pleases the chic persons who stay there and puts others in their place. My hotel is invisible from this roof, I am sorry to say.

Down below, at road-level, are the regulars, seated behind marble-top tables where they can watch life flowing about and comment on it. There is no notice here about having to buy *consommations*, but only the most important figures or friends of the *garçon-de-café* on duty can hope to sit long without ordering something.

In the mornings I use the Café de France road-level terrace as a writing-place. I have been coming here for the last two or three days, and sit writing in my notebook. At first the regulars looked at me, wondering what I was at for so long at a stretch. They did not want to speak to me, but they did want to know what I was up to. One of them, who knew some French, sat down at the next table a day or so ago, and regarded me. Finally he asked me outright what I was doing – in order to be able to tell the others, I suppose.

'I am writing,' I said. I didn't see why I should be more explicit. Of course my answer didn't satisfy him.

'Who are you writing to?'

'No one.'

'Then . . . ?' He sounded almost angry.

'I am writing a book.'

He did not believe me, principally I think because 'book' has a different sort of connotation here. The Bible is a 'book', the Qoran is *the* Book. The little French paperbacks that foreigners carry around and that one can see in the libraries aren't the same thing at all. He sat watching my pencil moving across the page and then turned away. After a while he went back to his friends and I was aware that they were whispering together. They didn't believe me. They were unbelieving to the point where it became difficult for me to believe it either – but I refused to stop writing on that account. They sat and watched me, these Moors with their three different kinds of face and dark inquisitive eyes. I suppose they were thinking that I was mad – but they accept the eccentricities of foreigners – at least, I think they do. They call foreigners *berraniyīn* – outsiders – regarding them as laughable and also pathetic. They are so safe themselves in the Muslim world that Allah has created for them that they can afford to patronize the poor, simple, underprivileged souls born outside it.

* * *

I have hired a bicycle – a very French one which tips the weight of the rider forward over the handlebars. It is more dashing but less comfortable than the staid English variety and it is painted in a modish metallic pink. The cycle-shop man wanted me to deposit my passport as surety, but this formality has been waived by the kind intervention of Moulay Ibrahim from the hotel.

The handlebars of my bicycle are curved, rather like the horns of Kaffir cattle, and the brakes are worked with cables which pass through long, flexible metal tubes. I have already learnt that a sudden snatch at the brake-handles is liable to disengage the cables and, when this happens, the bicycle makes an unexpected spurt forward. The saddle is very slim and elegant, sharp as a knife edge.

On this bicycle I have toured most parts of the city during the last few days, and also made a complete circuit of the ramparts. I can now understand why the fare tariff for victorias is so high for the *tour des remparts*. They are many kilometres in length. So far I have made little attempt to identify landmarks, except such as are already fixed in my head, like the minaret of the Koutoubia mosque. I would like to find the other minaret that seemed to me so beautiful from our roof. I shall ask 'Abdelqadir about it. Ordinarily, I content myself with demanding only the name of each *quartier* as I visit it; and then, when I get home again, I look up the *quartier* in the admirable town plan of my *Guide Michelin*.

I am losing all sense of direction and all sense of time in this city. You would think it would be possible to check the points of the compass from the way the shadows fall – but they fall in such an obviously haphazard fashion that it is not safe to rely on them. The set of the mosques in relation to Mecca should help too, but here again . . . Anyway, I disregard it, preferring to look up essentials in *Michelin*, but I don't think I shall bother any more. I have always had a very accurate sense of orientation. I still believe this to be true, but now know that Marrakesh lies outside normal rules. And why should I care where the North lies, anyway? It's just somewhere back there in the cold and sleet.

To make my tours guidebook in hand would be more rewarding, I dare say, if I were concerned with 'the facts'; but facts and names and dates and statistics hold no meaning for me until the things they stand for have become part of my life. I am a bad traveller. From a hurried visit to a new place, I carry back with me nothing but a general impression, difficult to put into words and probably inaccurate even for myself.

My object in bicycling in such discomfort round and round the city is to din into myself the shape and sound and smell of it. It will take months and months and then suddenly I shall possess the place. It will be mine – or in any case I shall have become part of it, which amounts to the same thing.

I told someone this the other day and he said it was nonsense. Nevertheless, it is the only way I can do it. Incidentally, it is also the way the Qoran is learnt, the 'perspicuous book' of Islam. Muslim children sit swaying back and forth in their tiny windowless schoolrooms while the preceptor flicks at them with his twig to hold their attention, endlessly repeating the verses. At first it means nothing, even the language is unfamiliar, but finally it takes charge. Once the Qoran has taken charge, the children are safely Muslim for ever.

* * *

Moulay Ibrahim has arranged Moghrabi-Arabic lessons for me from a friend of his. His name is El-Meknasi – that is to say, 'the Man from Meknes'. He must have a name of his own but he doesn't seem to use it. In a society where probably not more than a dozen personal names are commonly used, it is obvious that even linked with the father's name, thus – Mohamed bin Hamed, or Hamed bin Mohamed – a good deal of confusion must result. It is rather smart and distinctive to use a place-name or a tribal name as a clearer identification.

El-Meknasi was educated by the French, in Fez, and he speaks French very well. He is pleasant-looking, thirtyish, carefully dressed in the European fashion, with a tarboosh on his head. Perhaps he is a little too self-consciously enlightened, a little too urbane, but he is enthusiastic about his own language and knows how to explain its intricacies in terms of French grammar and syntax. We have had our first lesson. It was largely taken up with discovering how little I already know and checking my capacity to write the Arabic script. El-Meknasi says he is not quite satisfied with the way my European throat pronounces some of the sounds. There is a letter called *'ain*, for example, a guttural which involves retching far down in the gullet, and this torments me.

'It should sound like the bleating of a sheep,' he explains. 'Thus: 'a–'a–'a–'a–'a . . . ' and he bleats like a sheep.

I hope to be able to do this in time.

He is to come three evenings a week, and between lessons I am to write little exercises for him on the points covered at the previous session.

I noticed that he gave my room at the hotel an appraising glance. Does he consider it too mean for a pupil of his, even if it does belong to his friend Moulay Ibrahim? I have decided not to care what El-Meknasi thinks.

* * *

The air is vibrant with *Insha'Allah*. Wherever I go it is on men's lips, this phrase which admits the omnipotence of God. *Insha'Allah* – if God wills – I will do so-and-so; *Insha'Allah*, it will rain; *Insha'Allah*, Mohamed will return my packet of 'Casa Sport' cigarettes.

Resignation to the will of God and to what He may decide shall become of you is the very essence of Islam. It is no good making plans as if you were a free agent in the matter. No Muslim would consider trying. Any reference to the future requires that *Insha'Allah* should be added, and if the speaker forgets (which is unthinkable) somebody else must say it for him. This does not mean that a simple repetition of the formula will secure whatever it is that you are hoping for, but not to say it involves serious risk of failure.

Some years ago, in Waziristan, I was setting out by road for some place or other. 'We should arrive by teatime, I think,' I remarked to my driver, a Muslim. We did not arrive. Nothing particularly annoying happened to us – it was bad country, and it could be dangerous – but we had to spend the night in a place short of our destination. My driver was smugly pleased at this object lesson.

'Of course,' he said. 'What do you expect? You did not say "*Insha'Allah*".'

I knew the rules, so I said irritably, 'Then why didn't you say it for me?'

'Just to show,' he said.

I say it now all right. I even put it in telegrams announcing my arrival.

* * *

It was about a week after I had first started using the Café de France each morning as a writing-place that the regulars decided to ignore me. At first they had stared, then they only pretended not to stare and all the time I was conscious that they were watching covertly. Now they take me for granted. Moreover, they have begun to assume individual shapes and personalities for me, like shipboard creatures, and I feel compelled to nod good-morning to certain of them, particularly the grave old gentlemen who sit out their time in silence and alone, as often as not. They nod back, gravely and without warmth. Passers-by occasionally come up to these old gentlemen, mutter a greeting and attempt to kiss a hand or a shoulder which is as a rule snatched away before the lips can get at it.

Two or three times I have tried out a few words of Arabic on the less-exalted regulars. They reply in Arabic, or French if they can manage it. For the most part, their French is as shaky as my Arabic, and we have not yet dared to become involved in conversation. Probably they don't want to, and it is just as well, since neither party could get much further than the standard preliminaries.

And here is a curious thing: men who greet me today with apparent friendliness are quite capable of ignoring me tomorrow, though we may find ourselves once more at adjacent tables. It is both odd and in its way irritating. I don't care to be ignored when I have taken the trouble to be courteous, but it is a game for two or more players and I have started to notice my neighbours or otherwise in an entirely arbitrary fashion. My behaviour does not seem to strike them as offensive, so perhaps this is the convention.

* * *

If I were not so occupied with writing and with trying to make headway with Arabic, I believe I would sometimes feel very alone. Of course it should not be difficult to scrape acquaintance with some of the French people who live in Marrakesh, or with Moors who speak French. I have been tempted to do this, but on the whole it is best to continue as I have begun, and later, when my Arabic has started on the way to fluency, I can afford to relax a little.

I am frequently on the Djema'a el-Fna. I believe I know almost all the 'acts' by now and a good many of the *djellaba*-hoods that gather round them – by sight, I mean. There is a huge floating population in Marrakesh, as you would expect of this market for the great south, and at any given moment there are thousands and thousands of strangers in town. But there are hundreds of inhabitants too who seem to do no work and are always to be seen on the *place*. In a strange, inarticulate sort of way I have become friendly with a family of acrobats that performs every evening. It is only here that I see them. They wear professional costumes vaguely reminiscent of Tudor heralds, traditional for acrobats hereabouts, it seems. We just shake hands and bow and smile, and sometimes I give them a few francs. I have grown rather fond of the ostrich too. It stands so aloof in the litter of bones and beaks and eggs and feathers of other ostriches and makes no complaint when people stroke it or lift its wings in order to wonder at the little pink quills it has underneath. The by-products of an ostrich are much prized, though I am not yet quite certain what for – love philtres, I think. Then there is a particular snake-charmer I rather like, and a singer from the Sudan also. The latter has a stringed instrument, to the neck of which is attached a two-foot flexible metal strip with little silver coins ringed all the way up the length of it. He picks out the deep-toned Sudani melodies, and the metal feather quivers, producing a shivery *frou-frou-frou* from the little coins, like the movement of sequined skirts. Even without being able to speak to these people, I begin to feel a little less foreign on the Djema'a el-Fna.

* * *

I find it hard to sleep in this hotel because of the 'atmosphere', which is charged with a tension and the tension includes noise, but I can't pretend that the noise itself is excessive. Nevertheless, I sleep badly and I have been trying to turn my sleeplessness to account by studying Arabic grammar.

My waking mind grasps the triliteral root, that the consonants k, t, b, for example, represent the basic idea of 'writing'. I know that by sprinkling vowels – long ones which you must take the trouble to write and short ones which are but barely indicated by little flicks and stops and flying commas – that by sprinkling these vowels here and there, and by the addition of certain consonants, the various parts of speech are formed. It is very neat and very complicated, like the laying of the mosaics of which Moors are so fond, and I know now which vowels and which consonants, and where. I know it, but it requires a positive mental effort from me. I do not yet possess the knowledge so that my tongue and throat and lips produce the words without conscious prompting from my brain, and as I lie in bed battling with all this verbal geometry, my attention is distracted by the strangest of sounds. They are not alarming, nor even loud, but they trouble the air, and I can neither sleep nor study.

* * *

'Abdelqadir, the hotel proprietor's friend, has again asked me when I wish to pay the balance of the 'debt'.

I recalled our conversation on the first day when I had so carefully established the fact that Seigneur Hamed's debts are no concern of mine.

'But you are his friend!' 'Adbelqadir cried.

'No, I'm not.'

He looked at me slyly. 'Then you are his enemy?'

'Well, I am his friend if you insist, but I am *not* responsible for his debts.'

'Oh,' 'Abdelqadir commented doubtfully.

* * *

Although Moulay Ibrahim has spoken of me as his '*pensionnaire*', no meals are actually supplied in his hotel, so I have had to make my arrangements outside. After trying out a number of places, I have settled for a routine that is more or less satisfactory.

I take my *petit déjeuner* at the Café de France. For *déjeuner* I go to a little Greek restaurant where I can feed adequately for less than two hundred francs. And in the evenings I buy myself a sort of supper on the Djema'a el-Fna. Sometimes it is meat grilled on *brochettes*, sometimes a plate of stew. I get a piece of bread from one of the Berber women who sit in rows with Moorish loaves for sale. Looking round at the Moors, who are on the whole so well-fed and healthy-looking, I have decided that it is nonsense to start my life here with a fear of unnamed infections, and each evening I eat what I like and where I please.

On the way to lunch yesterday I stumbled on something very strange in a back alley, strange even for this city. A youngish man, ragged and only half-dressed, sat in the middle of the alley with his coat and pantaloons spread out before him on the ground. The coat had already been filled with charcoal and buttoned up, so that it resembled a stiff manikin, and, as I came by, he was busy stuffing the pantaloons with charcoal from a pile beside him. He was talking to himself and didn't seem to wish to talk to me, so I passed on, my questions unasked and probably unanswerable.

* * *

There seems to be an important and dignified group of people in Marrakesh – in all Moorish cities, I dare say – who make a living as intermediaries. They are called *Dalal*, or *Simsar*, and although most of them specialize, nearly all are ready to negotiate the purchase or sale of anything too large or inconvenient to be marketed in the *souqs*. Real estate, for example. One such *simsar* stopped me in the street, put me at my ease by explaining that he knew how dissatisfied I was with Moulay

Ibrahim's hotel (how did he know this, since I have scarcely admitted the fact even to myself?) and that he proposed to show me a little house which was available on rent, furnished, for a limited period. It belongs to a Frenchman at present out of Morocco.

'It has a *baignoire*,' he said, to encourage me.

A real bathtub with taps, apparently, not to mention running water, drains and electricity. It would certainly be pleasant to be able to wash comfortably at home. I have been going to the public *douches* in the new French town, but it is inconvenient to have to go so far. The *gardien* at the hotel has of course failed to do anything about helping with my admittance to a Moorish *hammām* in our *quartier*.

We have now been to see the house. But the man who was said to be holding the keys did not turn up at the rendezvous and during the twenty minutes of our wait, in a quiet, narrow alleyway quite close to the Pasha's palace ('very chic *quartier*,' the *simsar* pointed out), I learnt nothing of the house beyond the fact that it has a modern mortice lock in addition to the very *moyen-âge* keyhole in its front door. I was also able to establish that, whatever the number of rooms, one at least is at first-floor level with a window overlooking the alley. The *simsar* did not know the rent. We parted finally with expressions of gratitude towards each other.

Since then the *simsar* has been to see me and said that the man who has the key of the house has in fact not got the key, and this explains why he did not turn up on the first occasion. He was ashamed to come without the key. '*I* understand Europeans,' the *simsar* told me, and I suppose he meant that the man who had not got the key did not. Anyway, the man who really has it is someone else, a friend of the owner and also French. His name is Monsieur D—, or something like it, and he lives in such-and-such a street of the medina. So we went to see Monsieur D— together.

An elderly Frenchwoman with blue eyes and a fine creamy complexion opened the door to us. She did not seem in the least surprised at our inquiring after a Monsieur D—, though she told us his name was actually something quite different beginning with D. She smiled and was suddenly beautiful. 'He is at the other house,' she said, and turning to the *simsar*, asked if he knew where that was. He said he did; we thanked her and made our goodbyes.

When it came to the point, the *simsar* was uncertain where the other house was and I did not like to return to the first man to ask again. Yet it was useless wandering about the medina without knowing. The *simsar* was so nice and so unperturbed by our second failure – which, I admit, had wasted as much of his time as of mine – that I made no criticism. My time was my own, after all. I did, however, suggest that before making the next attempt he should inform himself not only of Monsieur D—'s true address, but should also confirm that he was likely to be there at a stated hour and ready to receive us.

'But naturally!' the *simsar* said, as if my suggestion were no more than obvious good sense.

'Who is this Monsieur D—? Are you *sure* he has the key?'

'*C'est mon camarade*,' he answered.

On the third attempt the *simsar's* arrangements worked like a charm and we found Monsieur D—'s new house. It is in fact a very old house and very beautiful. Moreover, we had passed under its walls on our way to make inquiries of the elderly Frenchwoman who, I now learn, is his mother.

Close to the Koutoubia there is a waste plot and to one side of it a wall over which the plumes of cypresses can be seen, stiff in the still air. The wall obviously encloses a very important site, here at the centre of an overcrowded city. I commented on this. 'Yes, there are many houses, many *riads* within,' he said. A *riad*, I gather, is an interior garden, a patio so large that it can be planted out like a formal garden. '. . . and orchards,' the *simsar* added.

It seems that the whole of this enclave is the property of a Berber family who are feudal landlords in the foothills of the Atlas and have for centuries enjoyed great power. The various members of this family – brothers, uncles, aunts, sons, nephews – have separate town houses here. There is a common entrance through the boundary walls of the enclave by way of a big gate, and beyond this is a meandering road that gives access to each of the houses in turn. Monsieur D— has rented one of the gardens and the pavilion in it. I had already noticed the pavilion, built close to the boundary wall, with a terrace overlooking the city, and another floor still higher. It was originally the *minzah*, intended for the entertainment of guests. But for three generations now no settlement and partition of property has followed upon the death of members of the family and, though rich in land and buildings, they enjoy only a fraction of their true revenues. Their homes are crumbling. Not one of them will maintain the house he occupies for fear that at the final partition it will be allotted to someone else. They quarrel endlessly. The *minzah* no longer receives guests and has fallen into shocking disrepair. It has been agreed to let it to Monsieur D— because he intends to recondition it.

Monsieur D—'s entrance is not by way of the big gate reserved for the family, but by a narrow tunnel cut through the wall. After the bustle of the streets it was strange to enter into a calm backwater full of fruit trees. A number of Berber women were watering the trees, building up little bastions of mud to deflect the flow from one channel to another so that each tree should get its share. A raised viaduct led through the orchard to the pavilion.

The pavilion itself is tall and slender, of pink sunbaked brick. It has a vaguely Mongol look, light in weight, with its features carefully defined. There are windows at orchard level, windows overlooking the terrace I had seen from outside, and the third floor has the air of a summerhouse, part wood with big glazed windows, part masonry. The texture is smooth and close-grained and the vines, the banana trees and little palms clustered at its feet seem to emphasize that this is the home of a people who are naïve but distinguished, and that the city has no power to touch the antique simplicity of the place. The door was open but no one was about except the Berber women in the orchard.

One of them called to us, 'Go on! M'soo Morruss is upstairs.'

The *simsar* led the way up.

The stairs take off from a small vestibule, twist to avoid a room at mezzanine level that would otherwise be in the way, debouch at the first floor, take off again in a slightly different direction, pause, duck under a beam, swing to the right, narrow, wriggle past a door that probably leads to the terrace and then suddenly widen, as if they were drawing breath and composing their features into the sort of smile guests use to accompany the taking of their host's hand. The top floor has been reached.

There are two reception rooms, *en suite*. The first is bounded on three sides by a continuous line of glazed and decorated windows, wood-framed, with two columns down the length of it. A double door leads to the second room. Its panels are deep blood-red outlined in gold of which the leaf has long ago fused with the wood itself. And then the second room, larger still, lit by a series of windows so low that the expanse of wall above them takes on a shadowed, submarine stillness. The place was in utter confusion, but even the chaos of chests, of divans that still awaited their covers, of lanterns, paint-pots, brushes, sacks of plaster and house-decorators' paraphernalia could not obscure the elegance of it. It was clear that the whole pavilion had been constructed to support these two rooms at a height from which the perfect panorama of the city could be seen. The first two floors were merely *dépendances* – kitchens, perhaps, vestibules for retainers of honoured guests, closets where dancers could await the summons. It enchanted me.

In the second room were two ladders with a plank stretched between them, and on the plank, very insecurely perched with a paintbrush in his hand, was a man of about thirty. He was obviously Chinese.

'*Bonjour*, Monsieur D—,' said the *simsar*, obstinately sticking to his own variant of the name. Somehow I had not expected a Chinese – and it seemed as if he had not really expected me. He was polite, but he was busy and didn't want to stop working. I stated my business as quickly as I could.

'Ah! *Bon. Bon*,' Monsieur D— said, and when he smiled his face suddenly became very beautiful and I was reminded of the Frenchwoman. '*Mais vous êtes mal renseigné, monsieur*. Monsieur O. does not wish to let his house – and certainly not furnished, since it is not furnished. The *simsar* was aware of this. I was told that you searched for a house to buy.'

I looked at the *simsar* and he smiled back at me in a friendly sort of way.

'*Quand même*,' Monsieur D— resumed, 'go to see the house if you wish.' He gave us the key.

We left almost at once. I don't think the *simsar* felt in the least abashed. I asked him why he had told me that the house was to let, and that it was furnished, when it was in fact neither. He said: '*C'est comme ça, paraît-il. Dommage*. We shall discover another, *Insha' Allah*.'

'What is your name?' I asked him.

'Si Idrees bin Ahmed.'

'Si Idrees bin Ahmed, if I had a pistol I would perhaps shoot you.'

He wagged his finger at me and said very seriously: '*Tch–tch*. Never.'

I begin to like him. He is fairly tall with a good forehead from which the hair has started to recede, and he has considerable charm.

* * *

My earlier impression that Moors have three kinds of face was accurate as far as it went, but I have now been here long enough to recognize infinite varieties within these types. You have the three basic faces – Arab, Berber and Negroid. And then the mixtures resulting from combinations of the three. In Fez, I am told, there is also a fairly widespread Israelite cast of face amongst the Muslims. This results from the conversion of Israelites to Islam which took place some centuries ago as an alternative to execution. It is said to have happened on quite a large scale. But here in Marrakesh this was perhaps not the case, so only three important racial elements contribute.

Though the skin colour varies astonishingly, Marrakeshis very often show one or more of the negroid characteristics – the fine, close-grained skin, the flattened nose, the lips protruding and smooth as sea anemones; the spherical rump, the narrow waist, the tight-curled resilience of the hair which grows on the head but little elsewhere. These characteristics may be watered down, but remain discernible. The explanation is of course that there has always been a regular import of slaves from the Sudan, and the children of slave women are as truly sons of the house as the children of a man's wives. There is consequently no social distinction based on skin colour. And since there is no social distinction, there is no socially-imposed attitude towards what is considered desirable in the human colour. Perhaps there is a tendency to prefer a warm brown to the cream of the Mediterranean or the alabaster of Northern Europe – and black is certainly held to promise passion. The dead white skin of the Saxon strikes most people here as . . . well, as dead white skin, and I must admit that under this African sun the Saxon resembles the fatty parts of cold mutton. On the beach even we prefer the effect of sunburn, after all.

* * *

Though I did not go a second time to see the Frenchman's house and instructed Idrees the *simsar* to return the key to Monsieur D— with a polite message, the result of all these abortive visits is that I am now determined to find some place to rent. I want my own front door. Until I acquire one I shall not belong in this city, and I have need of even synthetic roots.

* * *

I hate the primer from which El-Meknasi is trying to teach me Arabic. It must be intended for children – but do French children learn Arabic? Not as a rule, I am sure. Perhaps even an adult learning a language is expected to be content with the sort of vocabulary and phrase that these early lessons provide: Subject – verb – object. Very well. I agree. And tomorrow an adjective to brighten the image. But: ' 'Aysha (*nom de jeune fille*) has a *jolie* headscarf (*sibnīya*, fem.),' or, 'The slave-woman (*khadem*, fem.) works well.' I grow sick of everything being so *joli* and sweet and dutiful. I want to get on with life as we live it.

El-Meknasi makes me take notes on what I learn and when he leaves me his primer goes with him (he has other pupils, but only one primer, I suppose), so that I have no means of secretly dashing ahead to something more earthy. I have therefore bought myself a dictionary *Français–Arabe* and a new era has dawned for me. It is invaluable, this dictionary, full of examples to show how the various words are used, and of idiomatic phrases, adult and outspoken. So now with its help I write out sentences of my own composition and these I present to El-Meknasi when he comes to visit me. Today I had written:

> The lady in the green *djellaba* squeaks when she is pinched. She says she will complain to the Pasha, but the gentleman is unafraid.

El-Meknasi read so far with a disapproving deadpan face and then explained that 'squeak' is reserved for animals, and that the passive voice is best avoided. He also said that '*rājel*' (man) would be more appropriate to the context than '*sidi*' (which I had used for gentleman), all of which may be useful to know, but it is clear that he has missed the nuances. He continued reading. ' . . . "Mother of whores!" the gentleman remarked . . .' but he would read no further. A pity, because I had something nice waiting for him a line or two below.

I don't believe that he will ever teach me the language properly.

* * *

I met Monsieur D— in the *souqs* this evening. He was carrying a rucksack. Though I don't think he really wanted company, he suggested politely that I go with him to the auction sale in the copper-market if I cared to. I thought it might be interesting and agreed quickly before he changed his mind. I sense that he prefers to be alone but I find him interesting, this tall, slender Chinese person who speaks such beautiful French.

'Did you visit the house of Monsieur O. again, monsieur?' he asked me.

I explained the situation. 'I hope to find something else, furnished,' I said.

He is an *antiquaire*, it seems, and he is busy arranging his newly-acquired pavilion as showrooms. The copper-market is capable of supplying objects which he can restore for resale, he told me – though seldom of copper or brass, oddly enough. So most evenings he looks in at the auction sale. People bring whatever they have to sell in the way of household goods and furniture; the public bid, goods change hands.

'Do not hurry,' he said. 'Wait and finally you will find what you want. You want a *little* house? You will get one, but do not hurry. Time is unimportant here.'

I enjoyed the evening, though there was not much worth bidding for today. Monsieur D— bought an old wooden chest, leather-covered and studded with brass nails. It all took a very long time. A dozen auctioneers operate simultaneously, dashing about through the crowds in that narrow, closed market, shouting the latest sum bid for whatever they happened to be carrying. It was often a brass tray of the type called '*amara*, and the three utensils of differing but strictly traditional shape for sugar, mint and tea which are necessary for the ritual of mint-tea drinking. There were also elaborate braziers, glassware, old clocks, gramophones with horns, a perambulator, a table or two, watches, paraffin-vapour stoves borne blazing through the crush to show how well they worked. I am scared of paraffin-vapour stoves, but these did not seem to explode and I have noticed that Moorish mules do not kick, nor donkeys bite, so perhaps there is something in the Moroccan air that soothes the breast.

Prices are quoted in *reáls* which represent units of five francs – just as a *sou* represents a unit of five centimes. Moors more readily grasp the purchasing value of five *reáls* than of twenty-five francs. In France I can only with difficulty equate *cent sous* with five francs, so that I have the same sort of trouble with *reáls* in Marrakesh. Monsieur D— seems able to make the calculation automatically.

He is well known. He passes with Asiatic dignity through the *souqs* and is greeted formally but with friendliness. '*Lā bās*, M'soo D—,' they say, or, '*Lā bās*, M'soo Morruss.' His name is evidently Maurice. He achieves dignity and elegance with no effort at all. On his father's side he comes of an ancient Chinese family settled in Indo-China since the seventeenth century. He wears an old pair of khaki trousers and a khaki shirt and canvas boots. He is tall and thin. His hair, like coarse black grass, stands stiffly on his scalp in what is known as a *longue brosse*. He has a natural reserve bordering on austerity, so that the warmth of his smile, which he obviously gets from his French mother, is a surprise. In repose he is like a good drawing, very Chinese.

As we left the copper-market we passed a tall, grey-haired woman with high cheekbones. Monsieur D— stopped to say a few words to her but he did not present me. She wore a cotton dress, a necklace of coral twigs and had an air of such distinction that, when she had moved on, I asked who she was.

'Mademoiselle de V.,' he told me, without explanation. We had reached another section of the *souqs*. 'Here is the *souq aux tissus*. I wish to look there for a moment.' There was a large brass bedstead in the middle of the *souq*, covered with cloth remnants of all kinds.

'Does she live in Marrakesh?' I asked him.

He was not listening, so I repeated my question.

'Who? Oh, Mademoiselle de V.? Yes.'

A nave-like wooden roof with clerestory windows lets through the dying sun in shafts of light too high to touch the crowds rummaging about on the cobbles below. Monsieur D— was turning over pieces of cloth, examining a bit of brocade that had once been magnificent. I stood watching him. He is like a mandarin, I thought to myself. He smokes incessantly and he holds his cigarette in a very mandarin manner. I have never been to China, but that was the impression he gave. I also thought: I envy him his house. But I said, 'I suppose it's too much to hope that there's an auction for houses too?'

'But naturally. On Fridays, outside the principal mosque in each *quartier*. Do you want to buy then, after all?'

'Well, no . . . yes . . . ' I couldn't afford to buy a house, but I didn't explain this.

'After the midday prayers. What *quartier* interests you?'

I said I hadn't decided yet, but thanked him all the same. 'Is everything sold by auction, then?'

'Not slaves any more.'

'I suppose it suits the Moorish temperament.'

He thought I meant 'slaves' and said: 'Yes. They still have slaves – even people once rich and now poor still have them. The slaves would decline to leave.'

* * *

I don't want El-Meknasi to know because he would certainly interfere, but I have engaged a Moorish peasant to visit me occasionally for practice in conversation. The slowness of my progress irritates me. I shan't really be happy here until I can speak with some fluency, and until that happens I shall have to manage almost without friends too. Hence the Moorish peasant. This is a system I followed some years ago in learning Pashto (the Afghan language). It worked then and it may work again now. The peasant is for the moment a porter in one of the *souqs*. He is busy collecting together enough money to buy a woman.

I believe I have already made some advance – at least I am begining to string together words and phrases and I can understand more or less what the man says. As I can't make much in the way of extempore conversation. I set myself to prepare the main lines of what I would like to say and do my best to direct our conversation on to these prepared tracks.

The porter is a large, bundling figure, and he smiles very readily. His voice is clear and extremely loud, and his intelligence is so restricted that I needn't fear any very complicated or imaginative responses. I give him mint tea and cigarettes and fifty francs a lesson. He doesn't become bored because the essence of boredom is the dragging passage of time. For him time does not exist and so cannot drag. I don't get bored either because my mind is busy all the while. It is mental fatigue or my dinner-time that stops the lessons, not boredom.

* * *

On my way across the Djema'a el-Fna for an evening aperitif I was stopped by a Moor I have often seen at the café but to whom I have never spoken. He is obviously a respected person, and I have remarked that he gets served promptly by all the *garçons*. I have also remarked that he arrives at the café on a bicycle which has two little 'driving-mirrors'. These are fastened on the handlebars and I believe he uses them more for looking at himself in than to warn him of traffic coming up behind, because they are both tipped up into his face. He is rather a handsome fellow, as well as respected. Anyway, this time he greeted me as if we met regularly. I begin to manage the standard greetings fairly fluently now, unreeling my 'no-harms' and 'peace-on-yous' with quite an air. He suggested that we share the expenses of a lady wrapped in a *hāik* who was hurrying not very fast across the *place* in the opposite direction.

'Do you think . . . ?' I began, as best I could in Arabic.

He said, 'You want or you don't want?'

I started to say that I must look at my watch and consider my engagements for the evening, but by now the lady was hurrying back again at about the same speed and the man said urgently, 'You will pay her two parts and I will pay one part. Yes? I shall ask her?'

'Do you know her?' I inquired, still anxious to gain time. The lady was quite near now.

'No,' he said. 'But I will ask her.'

'I would like to see her properly first,' I said. She was completely covered by her *hāik* and I am not one who can judge from a pair of thick ankles. She looked like any other woman would look wrapped up in a cloth bundle. There was nothing to indicate her business at this hour and place that I could see.

'Why?' he demanded.

'Well, because . . . ' But by this time the lady was several yards beyond us again.

'You are as nothing!' the man cried angrily and hurried after her.

* * *

My encounter on the Djema'a el-Fna yesterday evening has set a train of thought working in my mind, and today I questioned El-Meknasi. I spoke in French because I wanted to make my meaning unmistakably clear. After recounting my conversation with the man about the woman, I finished up by saying, 'Tell me, monsieur, are *all* unescorted ladies admissible after, say, eight o'clock in the evening?'

He was angry. 'Certainly not!'

Then I said, 'You should teach me these things, you know. Speech and behaviour are so closely linked, after all, and you *are* my tutor.'

'What do you mean?'

'I mean . . . Well, I mean – is it not time for me to learn the language of love?'

He retired immediately into his shell. 'Attempt to say in Arabic,' he said in Arabic.

This is of course precisely what I am unable to do. Yet surely anyone can see that instruction is important to foreigners in a strange land, particularly in this land where there is so much free-floating emotion that no one can hope to escape all of it. It is like dust in the hair. Or rain. I must be taught how to comport myself in all circumstances – at all events, in the easily-foreseeable circumstances. El-Meknasi had already told me how one must make a half-bow and say, 'No harm on you, sir', or the response when someone gets it in first. He had also explained what should be said to a beggar to whom one does not propose to give anything, and about the gestures of modesty appropriate in a public *hammām*. What, then, should I have said to the man last night? And what to the woman? Why did the man cry out so angrily that I was 'as nothing'? What should I have done?

El-Meknasi was unyielding. I thought for a moment that it might be shyness on his part, so I tried to make things easier by quoting a few harmless examples from the English idiom to show what I meant. For instance, 'Were you looking for anybody in particular?' and, 'Pardon me, but could you please tell me the time?' – harmless, useful phrases with their established responses, indicating just as delicately as the questions themselves that one is perhaps 'waiting for a friend' there on the bench in the park, or that one has not got the time, one is sorry to say. I explained all this to him, and I think he was rather interested and would have liked to know more. Heaven knows, I was ready to tell him. But he suddenly drew himself up, returned his gaze to the wretched primer and said, 'Monsieur, I do not consider that you have yet made sufficient progress in the tongue. Come! Repeat! "The *sharifa* has a *jolie sibnīya*," "The *khadem* works well and is greatly attached to the *sharifa*." '

How in the name of Learning can I make the progress he demands if he continues to deny his help?

I shall try another way. I shall surprise El-Meknasi very shortly – surprise and, I hope, affront him!

*   *   *

I ran into Monsieur Maurice D— again today, and again he was on his way to the copper-market auction. This time he seemed to take it for granted that I proposed to accompany him, and I willingly did so. The quickest route from the point where we met is through the dyers' quarter. There is a small *place* bordered by a three-arched colonnade. Under the columns is a rectangular stone basin, a communal water reservoir to which animals are brought to drink or where water-carriers can fill their skins or men dip buckets. It must have been serving a thirsty public in this way for several hundred years. Beyond it, through an arch, are the dyers.

There are huge vats, of copper as a rule, and piles of cotton or silk yarns twisted into skeins. The dyes are of great beauty. In the vats they are sombre and concentrated. Where they have discoloured the hands and arms of the dyers, they take on the warmth of human skin; and on the tinted skeins, slung like grape clusters from bamboos across the width of the alley, they reach their apotheosis – green, red, gold, purple, enriched by the sunlight that passes through them.

'*Regardez les bambous,*' Maurice D— said; '*qu'ils sont beaux!*'

Stacks of them stood idly against the walls, waiting to be used. They were barely veined with colour.

Then on again, through a small *souq* where children's writing-boards of *thuya* wood are sold. The fragrance of *thuya* goes well with the filtered light. The copper-market is close by.

Fingering a brass chandelier in the copper-market, we again found Mademoiselle de V., this strange, serene personage with high cheek bones and hair grey before its time. Meantime, Maurice D— had told me something about her. She is, for example, a passionate collector of Moroccan objects: anything – amber, coral, silver, brass, embroidery – anything she happens to like and can afford to buy. The limit is set only by the money she can spare for luxuries, and this is so little that the objects she has already collected and arranged in a room she calls her '*petit musée*' must be accounted remarkable. She is of Caucasian origin.

I was glad to have this opportunity to meet her. Maurice D— presented me and we exchanged a few words. '*Vous collectionez aussi, monsieur?*' she asked. I wanted to say 'yes', though this is not true, but I was spared the temptation to lie because one of those currents that control the movements of crowds drove a wedge between us and we were temporarily separated. When I was able to rejoin them, Mademoiselle de V. was talking to Maurice D— about something else, in a very level voice, but one charged with sickroom significance. I caught the words, '. . . *paralysée, la pauvre*'. Her left arm was raised and she was passing her right hand up and down the side-seam of her dress. 'The leg is useless but somehow – *elle est tellement courageuse* – somehow she manages.'

Maurice D— said something that struck me as inadequate in the circumstances, but he is obviously a man who conceals his feelings. Mademoiselle de V. did not appear to notice this and was now making a formal goodbye. We parted. Then, a few yards away from us, she turned and called back over the heads of the crowd. There was a triumphant ring in her voice, '*Mais elle pond toujours!*'

She still lays! It was rather a startling comment. I looked at Maurice D—.

'She speaks of the chicken,' he explained.

His use of the definite article stuck in my mind . . .

* * *

My determination to surprise and affront El-Meknasi has cost me hours of preparation and some minutes of acute embarrassment. Last night I applied myself to compiling a suitable text – with the dictionary, of course. Today, when the porter arrived in a woolly cloud of *djellabas*, kicked off his shoes and slumped himself down on the windowsill, I went into the attack immediately. I am recording the conversation in English, though it took place in Arabic (a triumph in itself), and that is why it may appear a little stilted. I do not come out of it very well, but then neither does the porter.

'Listen, O Bouchaib,' I began, before he had time to complete even his greetings and get on with the news of the day, 'What do they say, the one to the other, when they desire to speak about Love?'

'Love?' He repeated the word I had used. It is one of two words given in my dictionary. The second, unhappily, begins with the letter ''*ain*' which is still beyond my powers.

'Yes. Love,' I repeated.

He shook his head slowly. I had anticipated a barrier of this sort and went on to my second prepared sentence. 'If, in the alleyway or upon the Djema'a el-Fna, you should see a person who is pleasing to you, and you should desire to make the acquaintance of that person, then how . . . ?'

To my disgust, he was not even listening. I believe he had been worrying over the word for 'love'. He suddenly interrupted me: 'Ah–h–h–h! . . . ' he exclaimed, wriggling with pleasure. '*L-Hwāya, yak?*'

This was neither of the two words for love to which I have referred, though, as it happens, in wandering idly through my dictionary, I have stumbled upon it under a different heading. It is not, in fact, a word that would be printable in English. 'Yes,' I admitted sternly, 'but in what words will we make this improper suggestion?'

He burst out laughing, a terrible conniving laugh. Then he leaned forward and, with a new familiarity, pinched me in the side. I could not be certain whether this pinch was to indicate the method he would employ or whether he merely wished to show his appreciation of a joke. He saw that I was puzzled, so he got to his feet and drew me to my feet too.

'Stand!' he commanded, placing me in the middle of the room. Then he pointed at me with a thick forefinger. 'You! You are that person!'

'Let us pretend so,' I said in French, rather primly I dare say. I had no sentence ready for this emergency.

He withdrew to the far end of the room. '*I*,' he cried, 'see . . . ' – his finger went to his eye which flashed tigerishly – 'YOU!' He pointed straight at me.

I stood my ground as he came surging forward down the room, a shambling, James Thurber figure. He stared first into my face, his own contorted with winks, and then at my ankles and, as he passed, he delivered a vicious blow with his elbow. I was left gasping as he turned.

'Understand?' he cried with a triumphant smile.

'But what do you *say* . . . ?' I began plaintively.

'Say? Say? Is not *l-hwāya* for *doing* then, in your country?'

'Of course, but . . . '

'*Wakhkha!*' he remarked, struggling to get out of the first of his *djellabas*. 'How much you give? You give me nice *favor?*'

I am afraid that the whole character of my relationship with the porter, hitherto so satisfactory, has been ruined by this incident. Of course I had to tell him to go at once. But I could not put things right for exactly the same reason as they went wrong – lack of vocabulary and the power to use it. He didn't understand, but he went, shaking his head like a poor bewildered ox, looking at the hundred-franc note I had given him for today's lesson and tomorrow's in lieu of notice. It is a great pity, because he was proving an excellent conversation man and I must now search for another.

* * *

I have been thinking over the 'house' question. I know now that not only do I want my own place but also, for peace of mind, I must very soon leave this hotel. Not that I don't like the hotel or Moulay Ibrahim or his friend – on the contrary, I like them very much. And of course it is cheap. A house will cost more. True, I don't care for the *gardien*, but his place is in the vestibule and he stays there. He does not really bother me at all; in fact he doesn't even say 'good morning' or 'good night' when I pass by.

No. There is something else about this hotel. I spend quite a lot of time in my room, writing or studying Arabic, and I simply cannot concentrate on my work. Such goings and comings below, whisperings, squeaks, quarrels, and once or twice the sound of blows. It is worse at night, but even by day it is bad enough. Once someone, very angry about something, threatened loudly to call the police. I try to rationalize the situation: I tell myself that Moors make a lot of noise about nothing, that after all it *is* their country and I had better get used to it as quickly as possible.

I would be less than human if I did not occasionally peep into the patio from my window to see what it is all about. What I see does not soothe me. Quite the reverse. I am living in a fog of other people's emotions.

Moulay Ibrahim and his friend remain phlegmatically untouched by it all. They just sit and play their game like draughts (but called '*dames*') and only look up from the board to collect payments.

* * *

The *gardien* came to my room this afternoon and said that someone was waiting downstairs to see me.

'Show him up,' I said.

'*Défendu.*'

'*Défendu? Mā fahemttk shi.* I don't understand.'

'*Défendu* by Moulay Ibrahim.'

'Moulay Ibrahim?' What could he mean? But it was no good trying to question so unwilling a witness. 'Who is it downstairs, anyway?' I asked.

'Si Idrees bin Ahmed.'

'Tell him to wait.'

When I got downstairs I found Idrees the *simsar* simmering with rage. '*Il m'a insulté!*' he cried. I took him firmly by the arm and pushed him upstairs protesting. When people square up to each other preparatory to fighting in Marrakesh, it is expected that someone else will separate them. There will be a token struggle, but they will submit – as a rule, in any case.

'*Tais-toi*, Idrees,' I said quietly, 'I'll deal with him afterwards. What have you come about?'

Idrees clattered up in front of me, grumbling to himself and throwing dark glances back in the *gardien's* direction. But when we reached my room, he turned and said brightly, 'A little house. Two rooms and *tout confort moderne!* Unfurnished. Rent is two thousand francs a month. *Tu veux?*'

'Where is it?'

'Derb esh-Shems.' And he told me the *quartier*. Not a very chic *quartier*, incidentally.

'Is it in good condition?'

'*Impeccable!*' he said. '*Absolument impeccable!*' I could see that he was delighted with the sound of the words.

'Let us look at it tomorrow,' I said.

'*Insha' Allah.*'

* * *

Things have certainly come galloping to a head.

Moulay Ibrahim and Si 'Abdelquadir came up to my room just now, within a few minutes of Idrees's departure. I invited them to sit down, which they did side by side on the bed and, after some minutes of small-talk and hedging, they came to the point. They said they had received complaints about me.

'Complaints . . . ?' I queried. I was rather taken aback.

'Yes.' Si 'Abdelqadir wriggled nervously, so Moulay Ibrahim laid a hand on the youth's shoulder to give him courage.

'*Iqul-uh. Zid*,' Moulay Ibrahim said to him. 'Go on, tell him.'

Si 'Abdelqadir swallowed and went on. 'There is a gentleman called Bouchaib, and he . . . '

'Bouchaib? Why, he's the man who has been coming to me for Arabic conversation.'

'So some say,' observed Moulay Ibrahim in Arabic, and then closed his mouth like a trap.

'*I* say it! Isn't that enough? What do you mean?' I was angry.

'My friend wishes to remind you that one is obliged to pay for *suppléments* in cash,' 'Abdelquadir said quickly. 'It is proper to come to us and pay at once, after such *suppléments*.'

'But I haven't had any *suppléments!* What is this talk about extras?'

'Sidi Bouchaib is an extra. And also . . . '

'But this is nonsense! Extras are things like – like mint tea! Or *petit déjeuner* in the morning, or – '

'Extras are anythings extra, monsieur.'

I was very nonplussed, but I controlled myself and settled back into my chair again. 'Go on,' I said patiently.

'*Eh bien*, monsieur, my friend Moulay Ibrahim wishes to remind you that you have not paid those charges.'

'I *am* paying the charges – at least I *will* pay them directly you send in the bill. The *full* official charges too, let *me* remind *you*. It's all written on the card behind the door.'

Si 'Abdelqadir took a deep breath. 'The charge for room-visitors is seventy-five francs for half an hour in the little rooms, and in this beautiful big room it is one hundred francs for half an hour.'

I looked towards Moulay Ibrahim who now broke into Arabic far too rapid for me to follow. So I had to turn back again to Si 'Abdelquadir, and he started to translate: 'Monsieur Mohamed the *gardien*, who is always sitting in the vestibule downstairs and never goes away so that he always knows and speaks the truth, has made the *calcul*. Even so Moulay Ibrahim from his profound love for you desires to accord a special reduction – but only because it is *you*, monsieur. You may pay only six hundred francs for the visits of this gentleman Bouchaib. El-Meknasi does not count in this *calcul*, of course.'

I did not quite know what to say, so I said, 'But *both* these gentlemen are my tutors in Arabic.'

'. . . And now the *simsar* Idrees tries to mount the stairs too! Anything is proper in this beautiful room provided you pay the correct charges and the door is locked and the other clients are not disturbed.'

This was too much. I got up from my chair and advanced on the bed. 'What!' I cried furiously. 'You dare to come to me with this nonsense!'

'Abdelqadir, who had shrunk back a little before the menace, now suddenly revived. 'Nonsense? Monsieur, control yourself!' He was genuinely shocked. He drew himself up stiffly and said, 'Monsieur! It is the *Code Napoléon*.'

I no longer knew whether to be angry or to laugh. In fact I did neither. I just sat down again, only vaguely conscious of Moulay Ibrahim's voice droning an Arabic accompaniment to my discomfiture. 'Abdelquadir was nodding and now began to translate: 'Moulay Ibrahim regrets deeply but he is unable to let you lodge in this beautiful room unless the charges are paid. Without doubt you realize that we are able to let it to others five times every night-time, and often twice or thrice every daytime as well, for twenty *reáls* each time – *more* even! It is from love of the cousin in Tangier and of you who are his friend, monsieur, that you are permitted to lodge for a simple thirty-one *reáls* a day.' He converted this into francs. 'For a simple one hundred and fifty-five francs a day.' Prodded by Moulay Ibrahim, he rose, took my hand and squeezed it pleadingly. 'Please to make the *calcul* and determine how much is lost each day on this account.'

Looked at from Moulay Ibrahim's viewpoint, there was no doubt that if the argument were accepted, the *calcul* was correct. Perhaps my capacity to understand this showed in my eyes. Anyway, Si 'Abdelqadir now returned to the detailed application of the rules.

'Monsieur Mohamed has made the *calcul* of the *suppléments*. He has a Dogma watch-bracelet, and he does not make errors. But Moulay

Ibrahim insists to make this reduction for you. You are obliged to pay only six hundred francs.'

'*Pfff*. . . !' said Moulay Ibrahim. 'Six hundred. *Kif wālu*. As nothing!'

'I prefer to leave the hotel,' I said.

'As you wish.'

'I will leave tomorrow.'

'*Wakhkha*,' said Moulay Ibrahim. 'But you will return to drink mint tea with us daily, *yak*? You must promise, *Insha' Allah*.'

'I promise,' I assured him. '*Insha' Allah*.'

There is nothing to be angry about, now that I come to think of it. It merely means that I shall be leaving sooner than I had expected. And apart from anything else, I don't like to think of Mohamed the *gardien* sitting there with a stopwatch.

3

Derb esh-Shems (I)

DERB ESH-SHEMS, *nimero* 4. The move has been made because some move had to be made at once, and so here I am. Things have not gone quite as I had originally intended, because there was no time. Moreover, the house has no water, though it proves to have electricity. I fetch the water every morning in two buckets, and do my best to make this quantity last for twenty-four hours. I ought to have a child's hoop or a wooden frame of some kind to keep the buckets from wetting my trousers. This is quite a problem at present, particularly because it has been raining. It ought not to at this time of year, but it has, and our street – my new street – is a sea of mud. The street is of course no more than good Marrakesh earth, trampled in by generations of feet, but at the extreme edges the surface slopes upwards and joins the shop- and house-fronts. These curving verges are the only parts on which one can walk dry-shod until the sun comes again to dry the mud, but they are too narrow to enable me to walk with a filled bucket on either side of me.

Derb esh-Shems – the alley of the sun – is not a very smart address, though one of the neighbours is said to have a lady relative who was once a Court favourite. There are no drains or piped water. The public water-point is in a main road that runs at right angles to our alley, near the ramparts. The pump is generally surrounded by neighbours' womenfolk – Berbers mostly, wives and daughters. It is an exclusively Muslim quarter and inhabited by poor people. I gather that there are, however, one or two grand houses overlapping from the smarter quarter next to ours.

The women at the water-point chaff me good-humouredly. Am I not married? Then why don't I get a *fiancée*? Then she could look after me. Who looks after me, who cooks? Must I really fetch the water myself? Why don't I get the water-carrier to bring me a skinful each day with his donkey? They don't do so, they explain, because the water-carrier charges ten francs a load and they have stout arms of their own. Look at them! They draw back their cuffs to show me. I have decided to take their advice and have gone so far as to ask the water-carrier to call on me. But either he has forgotten, or did not choose to come, or came when I was not in. His explanation is not very clear to me.

It is good water, this municipal supply, and drinkable. Fetching it takes about fifteen minutes, if you allow for the actual return journey, for waiting at the pump for your turn and with something in hand for the lengthy exchange of greetings when you meet neighbours on the way. Being new, and the only European hereabouts, everyone is interested in me. I have a great many neighbours, all of them with time on their hands and many who are still ignorant of who I am and why I have come to stay in their street. They don't like to ask direct questions all at once, so it takes time.

I was a little dismayed when I first saw the house. Idrees the *simsar*, who likes to please if he can, had not described it very accurately. In the special circumstances, I risked taking it without first having a look. But now I am in it I like it very much. I begin to feel that I have a stake in the city. I like my front door. The key is gigantic, incidentally – far too big to fit into my pocket, and this in itself has produced a mild embarrassment. It seems that to carry a key in the hand – as I must, for where else can I put it? – indicates that I am searching for someone to carry home to bed with me. 'I have a room and this is the key to it!' the situation proclaims. I have been told this by someone called 'Aysha, about whom I shall have quite a lot to say.

I have no furniture yet, except a mattress and bedding, two buckets and sufficient in the way of kitchen things to cook my food. A suitcase has to serve me as a bedside table. I have a room with undulating *dès* floors, white-plastered walls and ceiling, and a window in the front overlooking the alley. *Dès*, by the way, is a sort of alabaster-like surface made with quicklime and something, and pounded hard as stone. It has a wonderful creamy patina and when it cracks (which it does, quite soon, as a rule) it becomes veined as if it were real alabaster or marble. There is a very small landing open to the sky outside my room, and this serves as a kitchen, being provided with a plaster skirt over the place for the brazier. The plaster skirt keeps the rain out of the pot and also draws the smoke and cooking smells up through a chimney to the heavens. Stairs lead down to the entrance hall, and under the staircase is a lavatory of a very rudimentary nature. It is no more than a little hole in the ground with a brick on each side chipped into the shape of feet. I am already quite accustomed to it. As a matter of fact I have to back into it, my head bowed to avoid the undersides of the staircase. Underneath my room is a tiny shop belonging to a charcoal-seller. Quite convenient, I think.

Living in this house is very much like camping, but a good deal more pleasant because it is warm and dry (except in the kitchen) and there are no ants. There are also no mice since my assault on them during the past few nights. I have blocked their holes, too.

It is a poor quarter, certainly, but it does not smell at all; or, if it smells, it smells much as I do and so I don't notice it, as when everyone has eaten garlic. The only really serious problem that has presented itself is how to use my typewriter. Lying back on my mattress with a fat pillow to support my shoulders, I can manage to write in longhand. But typing remains awkward. I have tried using the suitcase as a typing-table, but this does not solve the problem of where to put my legs. Stretched out on either side of the machine, they protest, and ache. A proper chair and table are more or less out of the question in such a low room. The proportions of the room are designed, of course, for living on the floor and for feeding off a table of about footstool height (the suitcase again); moreover, the floors in this city are seldom true enough to carry a four-legged table securely. This is certainly why Moorish tables are so often three-legged. Three legs find their own balance, four don't, and wedges of paper are at best a miserable palliative.

Apart from these little inconveniences I am very content, and I shall learn to cook.

* * *

Though I am no longer in the hotel, for a time I still come each morning to the Café de France. My way now leads me across the Djema'a el-Fna with the sun in my eyes. I reach it by way of a side entrance, which is not the formal approach with its public gardens and post office (where Moulay Ibrahim was said to have been photographed) and the *Banque d'Etat du Maroc.* I come in past the hand-carts and what will later in the day be transformed into a second-hand clothes market. But in the morning, as I pass by, the handcart men are squatting between the shafts of their *charettes* drinking tea, because they have not long been awake. Some of them are still asleep, curled up on their *charette* platforms. There is quite a crowd round them, but not for custom. They are waiting their turn at the public wash-house behind – just the ordinary morning wash, not the *hammām*, of course. These are obviously people with no established homes of their own in the city: in from the *bled* (the word for countryside) stopping in *fondouks* and dosshouses where washing arrangements are inadequate. Later there will be another kind of crowd here, grouped round men who make a living with a type of three-card trick.

Beyond the handcart men and the wash-houses stretches the Djema'a el-Fna. It is the quietest moment of its whole day. At this hour the only attractions as a rule are snake-charmers (who need sun for their performances), one or two storytellers and singers in the Egyptian style.

* * *

As I crossed the Djema'a el-Fna I was hailed by the snake-charmer whose act I have so often stopped to watch. His assistants were busy preparing their tom-toms, passing them over a handful of flaming straw to tighten the drumheads. In a few minutes, when they were ready, they would begin to attract a circle of onlookers. They would probably choose the moment when the storyteller, with a crowd round him some ten metres distant, broke off his narrative at an internal climax to pass the bag round. The bag is his tom-tom generally. This would be a good time for the snake-charmer to start, because naturally everyone knows how the story finishes and would be ready for a diversion, not caring about the money-bag. At present, the snake-charmer's snakes were still in their box, under a lid marked MAHMOUD – CHARMEUR DE SERPENTS, and with a gay skull and cross-bones. Mahmoud smiled up at me, holding a paper.

'You are English? Read to me this letter in English.'

Everybody knows everybody else in Marrakesh. At least everybody knows everyone else who lives here – the tourists who come in for a look at the city and a taste of its delights don't count, except to have francs taken off them. So the snake-charmer knew me as a newcomer, in the vague way that I knew him. I took his paper. It was a letter dated some time in the previous winter from Bertram Mills's Circus, London, to say that they had no vacancies for circus artists in their coming season's programme.

'I have been in London,' Mahmoud said, watching me. He gave the name of city very round Os and accentuated the final syllable, Londón. '*And* Manchest*ér*, and Dub*lín*. Do you live there?'

I said yes, I did. It wasn't of course true, but what is truth? It was important to Mahmoud that I should live in those places, so that he could gain my sympathy for having been there himself. It was a sort of bond between us. Such bonds should not be broken, and Moors perfectly understand this. I proceeded to tell him in my halting Arabic what the letter said, and he commented, 'I know.'

'It is the biggest of all the circuses in England,' I added. And he said he knew that too. I don't believe it seemed in the least incongruous to him that he should play today to an audience that would scarcely scrape together three hundred francs before sunset – unless Americans came to town – and tomorrow . . . well, Bertram Mills, or Hagenbecks, or the Cirque d'Hiver; and the day after that? Who knew? *Allah i'aref*. The Lord God would know and decide about that.

So I was required to write in answer to Bertram Mills to say that

Mahmoud son of Hamed, *Charmeur-de-Serpents*, sent his greetings, was well by God's grace and ready to appear in their next season's programmes; that, as all knew, he was the finest *charmeur-de-serpents* and might peace and health attend the Circus itself. Meanwhile, Mahmoud had taken off his turban and his *djellaba* and was preparing himself for his act. He has a great deal of hair which he unbraids and lets fall over his shoulders. For his act he simply wears a white, cotton, sort of nightdress. The tom-toms were by now sharply treble and they were ready to begin. I told him I would type such a letter and he said thank you, and that he would sign it when it was ready. 'Put on the stamps,' he said, 'because I don't know about that.'

He was watching the storyteller all the time, and suddenly signalled to his assistants to start the banging. I left him and walked over to the Café de France.

* * *

Someone was making a '*ssss . . . ssss*' from the roadway, and I looked up from my scribbling. I had no reason to suppose the signal was intended for me, but it was such an urgent, unignorable noise that I had looked up automatically. Everyone else in the café was looking for the source of the noise too. The source was Moulay 'Abdullah: he is my landlord at Derb esh-Shems No. 4, and rather a nice little person, as far as I can judge from a single meeting. I waved to him and he came over to join me at my table, all smiles and good humour. I don't think he wanted anything in particular.

'*Lā bās?*' he inquired of me – 'No harm? – and I answered in the proper way. When we had completed the full exchange, I suggested that I order him a coffee and he said no, that he was just passing by and saw me, and then he started enquiring after my health again, with me responding as well as I could. Then he left me with a handshake and a courteous bow.

'*Ti connais* Moulay 'Abdullah?' The *garçon* was standing beside me.

'*Mais oui!* He is my landlord.'

'Ah! You have rented a *bīreau?*'

'*Bureau?*'

'Yes. *Bīreau*. You have rented it?'

I didn't quite follow. We were speaking in French and I understood perfectly what he was saying, but not what he meant.

'Where you write,' he explained.

'But I write here. Don't you see me writing every day?'

'*Oui, mais* . . . If people want you to write things, you must have a *bīreau* where they come and you write for them. No one comes here for you to write for them. I was thinking that Moulay 'Abdullah had come for a letter. I was saying in my head "*El hamdu l-llah!*" He commences to succeed!'

'But I told you the other day! I am writing a book. Don't you believe me?'

'A book . . . ?' He looked earnestly at me and waggled his head.

'Yes. A book. A *roman* – a novel. It is a book . . . about . . . ' I didn't know how to explain what a novel was. 'It is like the stories they tell on the Djema'a el-Fna, but not quite like. My book is about things that come out of my head, not things that my father has told me. I am *inventing* my story.'

'Ah . . . ' he said. '*Je comprends*,' and he looked over my shoulder at my notebook, shaking his head sadly. 'I cannot read that . . . Will you please tell me the story?'

'It is really a very silly story. Let us forget about it,' I said, and I shut the notebook.

'Long and silly,' he said. 'Will you please give me a cigarette?'

I gave him one. He smiled and went off to another table.

* * *

The conversation with the *garçon-de-café* was two days ago, but since then I get the impression that Moulay 'Abdullah's public display of friendship and the now-known fact that I have rented a little house from him has broken the ice, and that the 'regulars' at the café are thawing. They cannot yet quite place me, perhaps, but my association with the Moulay – who by virtue of being a descendant of the Prophet Mohamed is regarded as a superior person – helps enormously. I have already had signs of the change. Before luncheon, for example, one of the old regulars threaded his way between the tables to mine and sat himself down beside me. He held out his hand. I took it and looked inquiringly at him. He was behaving exactly as if we had known each other for years.

'Write, please . . . ' he said in Arabic, bringing a chequebook out of his pocket and laying it on the table. I was a little surprised but I filled in a cheque-form to his dictation. It was for a far larger sum than one might expect from the old man's appearance. He watched me writing all this and then grabbed the cheque-form and pen, and signed in very wiggly Arabic script. Smiling happily, but with no more than a suggestion of thanks, he got up and went back to his friends. I saw him showing them his cheque. After he had gone, a man nearby in denims leaned over and said, in French, 'That man is very, very notable. You know him? He is . . . ' and he said a name I neither recognized nor now remember.

Can it be that I have arrived?

* * *

Amongst my neighbours in the *derb* is a middle-aged Berber woman who tells me that she was at one time servant to a French bachelor. This explains her speaking French with such remarkable fluency. She is known as 'Aysha, though she says this is not her real name, and she is the one who told me about the significance of a big key swinging on one's finger. She is often at her door – just over the way from mine – and is much liked in the *quartier*. She has been helpful to me as a newcomer, telling me where to buy this and that, what to pay, offering her services if I am in trouble or need of them. She has also warned me very emphatically against the charcoal-seller whose shop is under my room. 'False weights,' she says darkly. But in this matter it is already clear that she has questionable motives. She wants me to transfer my custom to another charcoal-seller who has a shop at the end of the *derb*. I have said I will, but I don't think I will, for 'Abdeslem (the first-named charcoal-seller) seems perfectly honest to me and has been able to explain 'Aysha's real purpose. This he has done in a mixture of Arabic and French, the Arabic more comprehensible than the French, oddly enough. He has also told me a good deal about 'Aysha herself.

According to 'Abdeslem, 'Aysha re-entered and subsequently retired from a whorehouse after she left the French bachelor. She had put by a competence and is now able to live contentedly and alone, and can choose her partners instead of having to take what comes. She has presented the world at large with two children, possibly even three, though there is doubt about the third. Of the two known children, one is a boy and the other a girl. Both are now old enough to be on their own. The boy is said to be handsome, but the girl is not, and though 'Aysha's influence has secured her a post at her old 'house' in the *quartier réservé*, people say that she is not allowed to do more than swab down the floors. Anyway, whatever the situation, her children visit her from time to time, with little contributions of food or money. Even now that 'Aysha's professional life is behind her, she helps to supply a warm, bosomy sense of womanhood to life in our *derb*. There are plenty of other women, of course, but they all seem to be other people's wives or marriageable daughters and so on, and they hurry past with their *hāiks* pulled over their faces, so that they amount to not much more than an untidy reminder that they would exist if only they were attainable.

'Aysha pesters no one: she pays – or is paid – at market rates, as 'Abdeslem admits, and it seems that she has developed a powerful feeling for this handsome young man. He *is* rather handsome in the manner appreciated here: square, and bold-looking, with somewhat negroid features, though of the colour of burlap sacking. He has large teeth, two of them gold, the rest a brilliant white, and a very friendly smile which reveals them all. 'Aysha has probably been very pretty: she has a round face, bright eyes with a mark tattooed between them. She also has a tattoo mark which runs from the centre of her lower lip and down over her chin. She still seems to have a very good figure, but her charm lies in the astonishing vivacity of her expression.

'Abdeslem has no objection to 'Aysha's feeling for him – on the contrary, it was rather convenient to begin with, since she lives just across the road. He had no objection to aphrodisiacs either, though he hotly denies that they were ever necessary. What he does object to is that as soon as she learnt that he was bestowing his favours elsewhere as well, she changed her tactics. She began giving him magic possets which had a negative effect. He has ceased eating at her table, but the results of her possets persist, he says. He is justifiably annoyed, and has charged me with secrecy on the subject. He sits moping at his door, and it must be a great mortification to him to see 'Aysha rocking with laughter at hers.

'Must this go on for ever?' he cries rhetorically. 'Must I sell my dear little shop and go?'

I have counselled him to go back to 'Aysha, adding for comfort that she will eventually grow tired of him and will remove the magic. But my well-intentioned advice has hurt him deeply. His *amour-propre* is affronted to think that anyone should tire of him. Moreover, 'Aysha herself has recently been seen giving love potions to the public oven-man – everyone knows those little pink cakes she prepares. The oven-man has a new shirt. 'Absdelem has not had a new shirt for a very long time now. The man at the bicycle-shop told me this yesterday when he was pumping up my tyres. 'I wouldn't mind a new shirt myself,' he said.

Perhaps I had better speak to 'Aysha. Because of her friendliness with the French bachelor, she regards herself as linked with all Europeans and may therefore listen to me. I shall tell her that she is breaking 'Abdeslem's heart; or, in any case, that she seems to have gone further than necessary to teach him a lesson.

* * *

Quite regularly, in the evenings, I have taken to accompanying Maurice D— to the auctions. It fills in very comfortably the half-hour before an aperitif, and I find him interesting, intelligent and above all the sort of person I can meet and leave without having to explain where I have been and why I am suddenly going somewhere else.

Maurice D— wanted to buy an *opaline* in the form of a rosewater-sprinkler – he called it '*jette-parfum*'. Mademoiselle de V. was in the market again, still fingering the chandelier as if she had never left since the day she told us about the paralysed hen. She now told us that she did not think she would buy the chandelier, though her fingers continued to caress it.

'Is she laying still?' I asked her.

'*La pauvre poule paralytique? Mais oui, toujours*. But I do not believe that she will ever again hatch out little ones.'

I asked why.

'The *coq* no longer cares for her. Because she is afflicted. Is not *destin* cruel?' Mademoiselle de V. asked.

* * *

It seems that *destin* has been even crueller than Mademoiselle de V. had supposed. The unhappy fowl, which incidentally had been the gift of a Berber woman whose daughter Mademoiselle de V. had nursed during a serious illness, was until recently the only chicken in the run. She was linked by race, circumstance and affection to the cockerel. But today Mademoiselle de V. also possesses a turkey-hen and a well-bred *bressane* pullet which has started to lay. Mademoiselle de V. is ecstatic about these new arrivals which she has installed in aristocratic seclusion at the far end of her garden, behind a heap of stones. She speaks as if I knew every inch of her garden – which she calls the '*riad*' – and would at once understand, just as I would know about the little wooden pavilion where the *poule paralytique* has been segregated from her betters. Maurice D—, of course, knew all this, being an old friend of the household. Mademoiselle de V. then said to us – and here lies the ultimate cruelty of *destin* – that the *coq* has become very attached to the *poule bressane*.

'I find that there are elements of tragedy in your story, mademoiselle,' I told her.

'You think so.'

'I do indeed.'

* * *

'Abdeslem the charcoal-seller has to go to the *hammām* at least twice a week, and often three times because his *métier* makes him so dirty. He generally goes on Sundays, he says, often on Tuesdays and always on Thursdays so as to be clean for Friday, the Muslim *nehar edj-djem'a*. Living as I live, without a bathroom or the means of heating sufficient water to give myself a *douche* at home, without even enough water to heat for the purpose, unless I make a second journey to the pump, the *hammām* is the obvious solution. I asked 'Abdeslem if I could go with him. I have been struggling with saucepans of bathwater since I came to this house.

'Yes,' he said. 'I will speak to the *mul-l-hammām* and it will be all right.'

'Thank you very much.'

'*Wālu*,' he said. 'It is nothing. I will speak today and tomorrow we go, *Insha' Allah*.'

But when on the next night we went to the *hammām* he favours, quite near our *derb*, the *mul-l-hammām* looked rather sternly at me and said that Christians were not allowed. '*Memnu' l-l-nsāra*!' he said. Not for the Nazarenes. 'Abdeslem had evidently done nothing about softening up the ground in advance, and so a dispute arose. In general it couldn't matter in the least to 'Abdeslem, but he did very much mind that his own nominee should be refused, and that too in front of the others who were standing about in the entrance. He had to fight to save his honour.

As usual in disputes, everyone else present joined in. Some sided with the *mul-l-hammām* and some with 'Abdeslem – partisans from the same *quartier*, I imagine – but it was a *masseur* who finally tipped the balance my way. During the battle, I had had the good sense to engage his services and promise a generous *pourboire*. So we were allowed in.

It is not a grand *hammām* at all. The anteroom, where bathers take off their clothes and later sit around cooling after the bath, contains nothing but a broken-down bench along one side. There are hooks above it for *djellabas* and *camisas* and *serwal*, and you push your slippers under the seat so that thay are out of the way. Most of the hooks were occupied and a few men were curled up in cotton towels on the bench, dozing. 'Abdeslem motioned me to follow him into a corner. 'Have you a watch? Give it to the man. Have you anything else rich?'

We undressed down to our pants. Directly he was ready, 'Abdeslem made a serious face, drew his chin into his chest and started flexing his muscles to show how strong he was, in case anyone should be watching. Then he crossed the room to a pile of wooden buckets. I followed him in my pants. 'Take two and don't forget your soap,' he said. He took up two buckets. We pushed open a heavy wooden door and passed through it. A chain-and-pulley mechanism with a counterweight drew the door creakily shut behind us.

In the semi-darkness I could see nothing at first, but the place was filled with sounds, echoing and ricocheting round the walls. Men were calling to each other. I could hear running water, the clatter of buckets, a strange slapping noise. Gradually my eyes became more used to the darkness and I could make out a low, vaulted ceiling. Such light as there was flowed out from an embrasure, in a horizontal semi-opaque veil below which men lay naked and relaxed in the obscurity. Already I had lost 'Abdeslem, but he reappeared in a moment, carrying his two buckets filled with water.

'Fill your buckets,' he said.

'Where? Oh yes, over there . . . I see now.'

Steam was rising from an alcove at the far end of the room, and when I drew nearer I saw that there were two stone water-tanks. A man was already there, testing the water he had drawn. It was too hot apparently, so he dipped a second bucket into the cold tank and poured some into the first bucket. He had discarded the pants in which he had presumably entered the bath and, looking round, I now realized that everyone had done the same. I took mine off too. One feels ill at ease dressed in the presence of naked people. Then the man must have seen me standing uncertainly beside him and he took my two buckets, filling them without a word – one hot, the other tepid. I thanked him and went back to look for 'Abdeslem. A disembodied voice came from the darkness of a corner, ' . . . *dkhel f-is-skhūn*, . . . ' – he's gone into the hot. It was clear that I could still see much less than others who had been in the bath for some time. It made me feel doubly naked to be visible while they were not. I felt that my eyes, opened so unnaturally wide to pierce the darkness, must be big and frightened like those of a slow loris in the sun.

I followed round the sweating, discoloured walls looking for a door into 'the hot', and stumbled over a man. He made no complaint. Instead he got up and led me to the door. I noticed that he covered his sex modestly with one hand, as my tutor El-Meknasi had said was proper, and I wondered if I should do so too. I was unable to do so, however, since both my hands were occupied with carrying buckets. In any case, on thinking it over, I decided that it was ridiculous for naked men to pretend to be otherwise in front of each other.

The second room was a great deal hotter than the first, and larger, and the system of illumination was quite different. Here the ceiling was pierced by a dozen roundels of light, as if green-glass bottle-bases had been set into the masonry and lit from above. I think that is exactly what it was. Shafts of this light filtered milkily down through the atmosphere to the floor, picking out a torso, a pair of legs, a back – bodies dismembered by darkness and abandoned there on the stone. I looked round for 'Abdeslem but could not hope to recognize his amongst the limbs. Faces were indistinguishable, withdrawn somewhere in the shadow.

The floor was littered with bodies. Some were stretched flat, some squatted, many were being massaged or were themselves massaging their next-door neighbours. I felt stupidly shy. My skin seemed too white, and of a strange luminosity in this world of darkness and bodies the colour of dusk. I didn't belong here, and my sponsor was nowhere to be found. I longed to find myself a corner and to sit cloaked in obscurity, but the whole wall space was occupied and I could only stand unhappily, lit from above. Then I saw a door open and a further room momentarily revealed. I made for it quickly, before it should close once more.

This was the hottest room. My eyes were more or less used to the darkness by now and I was much relieved to find 'Abdeslem prancing about in the middle. He was shadow-boxing. Two or three men, squatting against the wall with their arms stuck stiffly forward over their knees, were watching him. Perhaps 'Abdeslem thought they were admiring him as he pranced about, feinting, covering up, delivering a rain of blows on his adversary, but I think it more likely that they just happened to have their eyes open, and 'Abdeslem just happened to be prancing there. He stopped when he saw me come in.

'*Fāin kūnti?*' he demanded.

'In the other room. I was waiting for the masseur,' I said, because I didn't wish him to think that I had minded being left alone. Moreover, it was true in a sense, though I had forgotten about massage until I said this and reminded myself of it.

'He won't come yet,' 'Abdeslem said. 'You have to sweat properly first. Sit down and let the sweat start.'

How welcoming heat is, if you surrender yourself to it.

I sat and sweated. It poured out of me. Finally the masseur came and pulled me by a leg, out into the middle of the room. One or two men against the walls watched me go through the hoop. The masseur proceeded to crack every joint in my body, and I lay there relaxed and let him do it. It was very painful. Then he sluiced me with water and took something out of his bucket. '*Mhekka*,' he said. I didn't care what it was – all I know is that it was rough and that he rubbed me with it. '*Shūf!*' he said. I tried to look: he was showing me the little rolls of dirt that had come out under the *mhekka*. I was faintly disgusted, but pleased to think that I would be clean when it was finished. More sluicing. Soap. I was sluiced again, and a final bucket of icy water brought me shouting to my feet and the masseur laughed gaily.

'Give me the soap,' 'Abdeslem said.

I lay quietly in the first room, exhausted. From time to time the doors opened – into the vestibule or into the hotter room. Once two opened in succession, huge doors which gave on to receding planes of milky, monochrome translucence.

Later still, I sat wrapped in a towel in the anteroom. The *mul-l-hammām* had mint tea brought to me. I smoked a cigarette. I felt that if I pushed against the seat I should go floating up towards the ceiling, light as a bubble. It cost thirty francs, plus tea and a tip to the masseur.

* * *

'Aysha sent her daughter round this morning with a message. I supposed it was the girl employed at 'Aysha's alma mater, and when she had delivered the message (which I scarcely understood, as a matter of fact), I asked her if she worked.

'*Iyyeh*,' she said, nodding.

'Where?' I asked vaguely, pretending that it really didn't matter at all to me, though I longed to know. She looked so small to be working, even if she isn't allowed to do much more than menial household tasks.

'*Ed-dar el-merhba*,' she said. The house of the Bienvenu. 'Abdeslem was peeping out of his charcoal-booth and called to her, 'You're getting quite big, aren't you?' and the girl nodded seriously. 'What have you come here for?'

I was glad 'Abdeslem asked this question because I hadn't followed exactly what it was all about. The girl repeated what she had presumably told me, and 'Abdeslem looked at me in inquiry, as if to ask if I had understood.

''Aysha is giving a *dyafa* tonight. She asks you to come too.'

A *dyafa* is a party. 'A proper *dyafa*? With dancers?'

'Very proper. You will come? I will tell the girl you will come, *yak*?'

'Of course I will come.'

The child was following all this and directly she heard that I was coming too, *Insha' Allah*, she said something softly and quickly to 'Abdeslem. 'Abdeslem nodded and turned back to me.

'What will you bring?' he asked.

'I shall bring . . . Well, what *shall* I bring? Wine?'

'Not wine,' he said in the voice of one who has caught another out in a social *gaffe*. 'Not *wine*. You had better bring chickens.' He swung round to the girl, asking, 'Chickens?'

'Abdeslem was taking so keen an interest in 'Aysha's *dyafa* that I wondered whether there had been a reconciliation between him and the hostess. I had heard nothing to that effect.

'Have you been reconciled to 'Aysha, then?' I whispered to him behind my hand. I have noticed that this is the polite way of exchanging a confidence in the presence of others who ought not to be allowed to hear. 'Abdeslem took up the pan from his charcoal scales to whisper behind and said, 'I shall come too, *Insha'Allah*. But don't tell them. I don't want her to make anything – *fahemti-ni*? You follow? – anything *spécial. Ti vois?*'

I said to the child,'Thank you very much, and may the blessing of God be upon you, my little love. I will come, if God wills, and I will bring for you two chickens. Tell your noble mother that I ask God to bless her.' I said it in Arabic without a halt. I was rather pleased with myself, and I don't think I have ever before managed to say such a long sentence extempore.

She smiled, pretended to kiss my hand, started forward as if to kiss 'Abdeslem's and then didn't after all (so perhaps the reconciliation is still incomplete), and left us. I think I saw 'Aysha's headscarf – the one with pictures of the Sultan printed on it in full colour – whisk back into her door as the girl went in. So probably 'Aysha had been watching the conversation. She generally watches everything that goes on in our *derb*, but I had the impression that this was important, because of 'Abdeslem.

'Who else is coming to the party?' I asked 'Abdeslem.

'I do not know. But I think there will certainly be the gentleman from the *Postes et Télégraphes* – the one who brings the letters. And his *fiancée*' [*fiancée* is usually said in French, and means something less, and yet something more, than in French] 'and also perhaps Sidi Bou Djem'a. And others who 'Aysha has known. Will you wear the *costume gris?* Yes? I do not consider that the *cravate marron rayée vert* is quite good for that *costume.* I was seeing you two days ago so dressed and I was thinking, "*Tiens!* What *dommage*! That *cravate* does not at all go with that *costume.*" '

'Do *you* want to wear the *cravate marron rayée vert* then?'

He had started to make a little pyramid of charcoal and now popped a big piece on top as a sort of cairn.

'*B–el–haqq*, I had not considered yet. But yes, if you wish. With my *veste en velours vert?* Is it that you propose?'

'I think *that* is what we had in mind, isn't it?'

* * *

It was the first time I had entered 'Aysha's house, and I was surprised to find how completely equipped it was for a party such as this. Of course she may have borrowed things too. The walls of the principal room were hung with *hāitis* and wherever there was space on the little tables she had put vases filled with paper flowers. She had also made paper shades for the electric-light bulbs of which there were two in the room, and a third which came in on the end of a long flex from the patio and was hooked over a picture-frame.

When I got there, I found, 'Abdeslem already seated on one of the divans. The '*amara* and *siniya* and tea things had been placed before him which most certainly means that he is back in favour. The senior guest is traditionally given the honour of making and pouring out the mint tea. He was busy preparing the first brew, but he found time to look up and make me a dignified bow from the waist. 'Aysha was rapturous, in layers of muslin dresses, embroidered with flowers. She also wore her gold-braided cordage and belts, a new *sibnīya* with bobbles on it, and a good deal of golden jewellery on her arms, neck, ears and forehead, and some on her breast too. I had never seen her like this before and thought she looked lovely. I told her so, and she pinched me on the behind and said, '*Mā shūfti shāy!*', by which I suppose she meant 'Just wait! You haven't seen a thing.' Then she introduced me to Si Fulan (*Postes et Télégraphes*) and his *fiancée*, a girl named Zwina who was behaving very demurely and didn't want to take off her veil till 'Aysha insisted. She was not very pretty when she took it off. There were two or three other men as well, one of them a big negro dressed in a black-and-white striped *djellaba*. He said his name was Bou Djem'a. Everyone was very welcoming and nice, and 'Abdeslem was by now starting to serve the tea. He had already tasted the brew in the special tasting-glass, nodded approvingly, poured what remained in the glass back into the teapot and looked round at us. A dozen little glasses of about the size and shape of the small tumblers used for claret in nineteenth-century England stood in front of him. They had rims decorated in various colours. 'Aysha came round with a plate of biscuits.

I dare say that parties of this kind always start very formally. Each person talked to his neighbours, and I did the best I could with mine – the big negro Bou Djem'a on one side, the *fiancée* Zwina on the other. They were very patient with my Arabic, and spoke slowly and clearly – at least Bou Djem'a did – so that I might understand; or perhaps this is the way he ordinarily talks. More people came in and sat down, but 'Aysha did not always introduce newcomers. I think that some of them were not considered up to much socially. I thought I saw the water-carrier, for example, but when I looked again he had gone. Perhaps I was mistaken. 'Aysha's two children were acting as servers and I expect there was some slaveling outside in the little patio, to keep the braziers going and to help serve.

For the dinner we had to group ourselves round two or three circular tables drawn up to the divans, managing as best we might. I could see that, with all the will in the world, my two chickens could not feed the party, and when food came it proved to be a sort of *tajīn* – beef stewed with black olives and *poivrons*. Not bad, but I wondered about my chickens. A second dish arrived after the *tajīn* and this time it *was* my chickens, stewed with rounds of lemon. The other tables were being given something else which I could not clearly see. Finally *couscous*. I have eaten *couscous* in Paris and been told that it would be much better in North Africa. Now I have eaten it in Morocco and I think that probably it must be much better in Algeria or somewhere else. It seems to me that semolina is always less good than rice, even indifferent rice, and the meat accompaniment was unremarkable. We finished the dish, all the same.

It was a filling meal all right. We sat back contentedly. We had eaten with our fingers in the ordinary way, the fingers of the right hand. Si Fulan's *fiancée* had done so with tremendous gentility, and when she had finished there was scarcely any grease on her at all. What there was she managed to clean off with no more than a couple of ladylike licks and then sat with her hands held together in front of her to let them dry out. Bou Djem'a was different. I watched entranced as he worked a huge pink tongue round and round his knuckles. He saw me watching and smiled comfortably.

'*Meziān*,' he remarked, examining his fingers.

Then sweets: big, black slabs like fudge, and a *gâteau* very similar to *millefeuilles* but oozing with honey. The sweets were really the best part of the meal, I think, and I took more of the fudge, to Bou Djem'a's amusement.

'*Meziān oula la?*' he asked. It was good, and I said so. 'But I prefer when it is more sugared,' he went on. 'When you come to my house you shall see. My woman makes *nīmero wāhad*.' Number one: first class! 'Abdeslem caught my eye from the next table, nodding as 'Aysha offered me still more. But there is a limit after all, and I said, 'No thank you. Later perhaps.' They were bringing round a ewer and a basin with towels and soap and we all cleaned ourselves up.

Even before they served the next glass of mint tea someone had taken out a stringed instrument and was tuning it. Nobody had asked him to play, as far as I know, but it was reasonable that he should. It was a little two-stringed instrument, both strings tuned to the same note. The body was pendant-shaped, wood probably, covered with coarse hide. Si Fulan's *fiancée* leaned across me to say something confidential to Bou Djem'a and, in doing so, stamped on my foot. I moved it, and she stamped again, so I wondered if after all she had meant it the first time. Bou Djem'a whispered back to her and everyone looked their way. But Si Fulan seemed quite unperturbed about it. Meanwhile the musician had started to sing.

It was less a song than a story, and the music was less music than an intermittent twanging to mark pauses between stanzas, or simply when the singer wanted a rest, like on the Djema'a el-Fna. Tea was on its way round again. Everyone sipped it with a great intake of breath, partly because it was so hot and partly because it is considered better taken this way – just a few drops at a time and a great deal of air.

In the middle of the song and the tea-drinking some more guests arrived, amongst them the night-watchman of our *derb* and a girl who, on taking off her *hāik*, was so pretty that we all stopped sipping to look. The *fiancée* gave a tiny little snort. Even the singer stopped. Bou Djem'a quite frankly said, 'Ah–h . . . !' very loudly indeed, followed by some kissing noises.

'*Halwa? Zid, jbed shuwīya,*' the *fiancée* said softly, holding out the plate of sweetmeats. '*Hādak. El-kāhla . . .* ' She picked up a piece of the black fudge and gave it to me, smiling. I took it and thanked her. The singer had started a new song and Si Fulan stretched across the *fiancée* saying: '*C'est une autre chanson. Une nouvelle.* I will tell you what he is singing.' He speaks quite passable French and off he went, a sentence or so behind the singer.

'From a city of the cities of el-Moghreb a voyager set out on his way to Marrakesh. He was poor but vigorous, and he walked all day across plains and little hills with no thought for beasts or robbers because of the singing in his belly . . . '

'Do you like Si Fulan's *fiancée*?' Bou Djem'a whispered to me.

'No. Not much.'

'Neither do I. She is too thin. Look at her! Too thin.'

'I don't want to look at her.' I was looking at the new girl, as a matter of fact, and Bou Djem'a noticed this.

'*That* is the good one. *Meziāna! Hādak Meziāna*,' and he made more kissing noises. I tried to stop him, but he paid no attention, and Si Fulan was prodding at me across the *fiancée*. 'Listen,' he was saying: '. . . But by eventide when the sun left the world and all became darkness the voyager was weary and perhaps frightened too . . . '

'Abdeslem had left the room a moment before and now returned, but, instead of going back to his seat, he shamelessly wedged himself in between the new girl and the night-watchman. I could see that 'Aysha was not pleased.

'. . . lamplight flowing from a window,' continued Si Fulan, raising his voice slightly to drown the very indecent noises that Bou Djem'a was now aiming across to the far divan. 'The voyager entered. "I wish of God and of you," said he to the widow woman, "to eat and to drink and to rest for the night, for I have voyaged all day without sustenance." '

'Give me a *halwa*,' Bou Djem'a hissed at me, but without looking. I stretched for the plate and he took two. One he popped straight into his mouth and the second he thrust vaguely in the direction of mine, still without looking. I ate it out of politeness and then turned back to Si Fulan in answer to his tweaking. He seemed mildly annoyed at my divided attention and allowed it to show in his voice, though it did not at all suit the context: ' "Alas, I have nought but these chickens that you see," replied the widow woman, pointing about the hut, "and the three boiled eggs that even now complete their cooking upon the fire." "*Merci beaucoup*," remarked the voyager and he took and ate the three eggs.'

I saw with interest that 'Aysha had beckoned away the night-watchman and that he now came back to the divan, smacked the new girl on the leg and quickly slipped into the space beside her while she was recoiling from the blow. It was stuffy in the room, but I was very content. In fact I felt wonderful, and I thought the new girl looked wonderful too, warm, and such big brown eyes – would they be brown? I was uncertain at that distance – big, anyway. I think I started to tell Bou Djem'a about it. I wanted to make some sort of plan, but Si Fulan was really being tiresomely exacting: 'You must listen. *Vous êtes obligé à m'entendre! Voyons!*'

'He does not wish to listen,' the *fiancée* said coldly to him. 'He is watching that little *qahba*.'

'*Qahba*,' murmured Bou Djem'a contentedly.

'Next day the voyager thanked the widow woman, made his farewell and left on his journey to Marrakesh and after several years he became rich and important whereas the widow woman remained poor.'

'Good,' I said, without thinking.

'Good? What can you mean?' Si Fulan was indignant.

'I'm sorry,' I said. 'I meant "Bad". I'm very sorry.' I don't know what had come over me. I felt as if I might start laughing soon and I searched my brain for the funny circumstance that was responsible. 'I can't think,' I said – or something of the sort.

'You have only to listen,' Si Fulan said sternly. 'You have eaten too much *halwa*. That's what it is.'

My brain was getting clearer and clearer. I saw exactly what sort of plan I had to make. I think I squeezed the *fiancée* a little in order to console her for being so thin and plain when the new girl was so beautiful, and, momentarily inattentive, I did not notice that Bou Djem'a had slipped away on hands and knees. It was only when I turned to outline my plan to him that I found him gone. He was several yards away by now and my blood was up. Treachery! I jumped up, flew across the room and brought him back. I was of course very powerful at the time.

'He is crying,' the *fiancée* said morosely, nodding towards Bou Djem'a, and it was true. 'I tire of these tears. Men,' she said. '*Men*. Even a little piece of *halwa* is stronger than a man.'

Si Fulan had been droning on all this time and suddenly realized that I had not heard. He was very angry.

'You are missing the fine part!' he cried. 'Have you heard how an enemy of the voyager-now-rich goes to the widow and causes her to complain to the Pasha? Have you heard?'

'No. I'm sorry. I seem to have been very busy lately. But what had she to complain of? And what have *you* to complain of, Si Fulan?' My voice sounded very loud.

'Hush,' he said placatingly. 'Nothing for me. But *she* had. The enemy of the now-rich voyager makes her to complain to the Pasha in this way: "O sir, think of my riches gone! Think of my three little eggs from which would have emerged chicks, and think of the eggs they too were waiting to lay, and the more chicks, and this throughout the years that this rich man is being rich in Marrakesh and me poor in my hovel. Think!" '

'The fine part is now coming,' said the *fiancée.*

Was I mistaken? Was she speaking French? Could she?

'Good,' I said politely. The new girl seemed to be looking up sideways at 'Abdeslem across the night-watchman, and 'Abdeslem's arm was stretched across the night-watchman's shoulders as far as her neck, which I was certain could mean no good for anyone. 'You had better tell 'Aysha,' I whispered to Bou Djem'a, but unfortunately Bou Djem'a was sleeping. We did not like to disturb him.

' . . . "Where is the defendant?" cried the Pasha!' Si Fulan was making a glorious effort. ' . . . 'But where is the defendant?' A man stepped forward very neat and said, "By your leave I am sent by the defendant to say he is unable to come today." "And why?" asked the Pasha. "Because he is gone to his fields," the neat man replied. "What does he in those fields?" "I think, monsieur, that he is at planting out boiled beans so that he may reap a rich harvest in the years to come-richer even than from boiled eggs!" Thereupon the Pasha laughed heartily and dismissed the case.'

Bou Djem'a had woken and said, '*Halwa.*'

'Do not give,' the *fiancée* muttered. 'Already he is useless with *halwa.*'

Si Fulan was beaming at me through the mist that had arisen in the last few minutes. 'Now tell me how you enjoyed the story, monsieur,' he said, but somehow, nice as he was, I had no wish to speak to him. I wished to speak to the new girl. I don't exactly remember the sequence of events – whether perhaps it was now that I danced a slow romantic valse in the costume of a Hussar; there was certainly a horse somewhere, and flashes of fire – from the horse's nostrils, probably. And Bou Djem'a behaved rather badly in some way that I now forget, something to do with the *fiancée*, I fancy, though possibly that was later, and not Bou Djem'a at all. Much later. I am uncertain of the time . . .

* * *

I awoke late this morning, fresh as a daisy but disorientated. I am sorry to say that the *fiancée* was there, and that actually it was she who woke me. I don't really like her very much and I cannot think how it came about that she was in my house at all, but she was, and when she brought me my mint tea, she gave a smacking kiss and said: '*Min dāba kull sbah nesaub-lek atay, yak*?' which means that henceforth this *fiancée* whom I don't in the least care about intended to wake me each morning with a pot of mint tea. I looked round for Si Fulan but he did not seem to be there.

'Where is Si Fulan?' I asked her reprovingly.

'*Ikūn f-id-dar dyāl-uh* . . . He must be in his house. I am *your fiancée* now.'

She looked awful in the light of day – but then I dare say that I did too. I didn't quite know what to do about it. And what about Si Fulan? Would he be pleased? I had to consult with 'Aysha quietly, perhaps with 'Abdeslem too. Between them they would know how to deal with such a situation. What had happened to the 'new girl', incidentally?

'Give me money and I will buy *svenj*,' the *fiancée* was saying. *Svenj* are little *beignets* in rings and I cannot say how much I disliked the thought of them. But I thought too that once she were out of the house – on this loving errand, for example – perhaps it would be easier. So I gave her money.

'The *svenj* I prefer are to be purchased from a stall opposite the *tabac* on the Djema'a el-Fna,' I told her. Somehow my tongue did not seem to get round the Arabic words as well as it ought. Last night there had been no difficulty at all.

She had the effrontery to pout, 'What a long way . . . '

'Never mind, my little love,' I said. 'You have good strong legs.' She has, too. She had hitched up her overskirts, for housework I suppose, and I could see them. She took the money and went.

Directly I heard the front door shut, I hurried out of bed and ran downstairs. Bou Djem'a was lying asleep in the vestibule. On the floor. This was getting too much. I went into the alley. 'Abdeslem's charcoal-shop was shuttered. 'Aysha's door was closed too, but I crossed and knocked on it. Neighbours were passing and smiled at me, and one of them laughed outright. Then 'Aysha came to her door.

Thank God for 'Aysha! She is wonderful. She said that I might leave the *fiancée* to her – and Bou Djem'a too, and that would be the end of it, but . . . her lips tightened.

'You know about 'Abdeslem?' she asked.

'No. What about him?'

'And that little *putain* who came with the night-watchman? You do not know?'

'How should I know?'

'That girl is already with the Pasha's police because she is entirely without authority and must be punished. And 'Abdeslem is . . . well, 'Abdeslem . . . I have had to give him some little possets . . . You are aware of these possets . . . ? Yes, I thought you would know. Possets, and some rather particular powders and . . . A Berber lady helped and advised. It was necessary to hold 'Abdeslem down like a chicken that is to be filled. Friends very kindly assisted. If you require charcoal today, *cher* Monsieur Peter, I must ask you to go to the *brave homme* at the end of our *derb*. It seems that 'Abdeslem's *boutique* is locked from the outside . . . ' Slowly she wiggled a key on the end of a string. 'You enjoyed the *dyāfa*, yes? Bou Djem'a also makes good *halwa* – he uses the *hashshish* from his *bled*: he pretends it is better. But mine also is good, yes?'

Derb esh-Shems (2)

I AM RESOLVED never to run, to walk always with a slow, measured tread, and that when I choose, or am actually compelled, to look to right or left, I shall do so calmly and tranquilly. I shall gear down my jittery European reactions to those of a Blue-man riding his camel across the Mauretanian deserts. I shall refuse to be hustled – why hurry? All the evidence about me points to the fact that it is for ever NOW. You can't go skipping into the future, however much you hustle. I shall be content, as the Moors are, with me in the centre of my universe and leave the universe to do the spinning.

The last few days have been trying. The *fiancée.* 'Aysha did her best, I am sure, and perhaps part of what happened was my fault, because when I went back to my room to sleep in the comfortable knowledge that everything had been left in her hands, I forgot to turn the key in the front door and also forgot that the *fiancée* had her own plans. She returned with half a dozen *svenj* looped on a piece of string and she was in my vestibule before 'Aysha could get at her. Then I heard them fighting down below – in the vestibule – and Bou Djem'a seems to have come out of his swoon and started lashing about too, and so a crowd collected and some members of the Pasha's police and – well, I don't propose to think any more about it. It cost more money than I can afford, because the *fiancée* pitched her demands a good deal higher than anyone could have guessed from looking at her. And so on. She was eventually taken away and I could hear her screaming as I clambered back into bed. My male neighbours say that I behaved in an exemplary fashion, but the women (except 'Aysha) sided with the *fiancée* at first, on principle. They have come round since, I am glad to say.

Bou Djem'a says he will only be staying for a few days, and I would have said that the few days had already passed.

* * *

'Abdeslem has disappeared completely. No one knows where he has gone, and that is really why 'Aysha has been too busy with her own affairs lately to see her friends. His shop-front was found broken open late on the very day that she had locked him inside. No one saw or heard a thing, and 'Aysha is believed to have complained to the lady who had supplied the powders. We went to examine the shop, and I think some were disappointed to see that the charcoal stocks had been moved too. Naturally suspicion falls upon the night-watchman – not of having stolen the charcoal, but of collusion with 'Abdeslem. But since the 'new girl' was the night-watchman's protégée, and 'Abdeslem had . . . Or have we got it all wrong? Was the night-watchman just helping the 'new girl' on her way up the social ladder the night of 'Aysha's *dyāfa*? Had 'Aysha really put down something quite substantial on account, in order to win back 'Abdeslem's waning affections? Did 'Abdeslem chivalrously hand over part of this offering to the 'new girl'? Some of the neighbours hold this theory, but I don't know. The night-watchman affects to be very worried indeed about it all, because he says that the 'new girl' can't be found either. 'And who is going to pay?' he asks.

* * *

The days are going by in this endless 'now' and I have managed to get a good deal of writing done. Bou Djem'a left some time ago. He just went out one day and never came back. He really is very nice – no trouble at all, and even helpful in some ways, cooking and fetching water and so forth. He has made rather a mess in the 'kitchen', however. He had to cook his *hashshish*, I quite understand that, and naturally it involves all sorts of sticky ingredients to make it nice – sugar and spices – and a lot gets stuck on the floor and walls. He used to bring me pieces of it, but I really think I can do without.

A little money has come in, which is welcome. Every now and then I force myself to examine my bank balance. It doesn't give me any pleasure – even when it enables me to see six months ahead – except the purely negative pleasure of deciding not to think about it again for that period of time. But it is capable of giving me pain. My credit balance has been painfully thin lately. I was thinking only the other day that I must do something about it. It has been sinking all the while, without my realising it.

How can I make money and yet continue to live? That is my problem. Living means leisure and leisure is exactly what a job denies you. Moors know this and pop in and out of jobs as their stomachs are empty or full, but I am still a long way from reaching that happy state. They don't care what happens and in any case are satisfied that God will determine their futures as He pleases. So they don't have to strive for success, and this is what makes living amongst them such a wonderful relief. For them, none of the things that befall you can be disgraceful because, good or bad, everything comes from God. With us, it is somehow disgraceful to be poor, no matter how we protest to the contrary, because poverty suggests failure. Hence the struggle to keep up appearances and, when that doesn't come off, trying to keep your end up, and then, rather hopelessly, just keeping your head above water. In Marrakesh, you can be poor and rich in turns and nobody seems to notice the difference except in unimportant ways. Your clothes get shabbier perhaps, and then suddenly you have a new outfit. When that happens, the others are expected to congratulate you on your new clothes – '. . . *b-sahht-ek . . . el-keswa . . .*'

But for the present some money has come in. I have so little talent for money that I shall never make a success of it. You need talent for it, just as you need talent for painting or music or writing. You have to have just a little bit of the *feu sacré* to love money and make it.

* * *

It has become much hotter recently. Midsummer is past, even my birthday on the 12th of July, which I probably would not have remembered had it not been marked by special letters from my family.

*   *   *

Last night I had an opportunity of seeing *la poule paralysée* for myself. Mademoiselle de V. had invited me to join '*une petite réunion de nos amis*' and I gladly accepted. We really scarcely know each other and it was a kind gesture to include me amongst her guests.

I find that her front door is already familiar to me. It is the little scarred wooden door with the number five painted upside-down above it (or is it a 'two' backwards?) that I have noted when bicycling through a remote *quartier* of the city. The door is set in an immense wall, which makes the alleyway skirting it appear even narrower than it is. Actually, there is room in the alley for two bicycles to pass, plus a pedestrian flattened against the wall. I went to the house with Maurice D—.

The door stood ajar, waiting for us, back-lit by a Moorish lantern. Visitors have to creep through the low door on all fours, and beyond it the *riad* was a pool of darkness with but one other point of illumination – a second lantern hanging low in a tree. Mademoiselle de V. was sitting under the second lantern with her other guests, but in such a fashion that none of the light shining outwards through the coloured-glass panels fell directly upon her. She was in the shadows till she heard our arrival and then rose to greet us, coming forward barefoot over the rough ground of which, I suppose, her feet knew every little stone. As she came within range of the vestibule lantern, I was struck by her beauty, the smooth, placid beauty of an eighteenth-century portrait, very formal, very un-pin-up; the calm blue eyes, the lashes and brows quite unaccented, the clear skin, the architecture of the bones, the peace and serenity of it. It has nothing to do with Coca-Cola. The fact that her hair is apt to escape from its fastenings, and had done so last night, is not of the least significance.

She led us through the *riad*. It has a hidden, labyrinthine quality. I was then introduced to the others and we sat and talked. Each of us had a stool set about a low, circular Fez table. There was a strangely eclectic display of glassware, some of it very good and presumably from her 'museum'. There was also a bottle of 'Old Lady's Gin' and another of

Cinzano. For some reason, Mademoiselle de V. supposed that I would know how to make a cocktail with these ingredients and no ice, and she asked me to do so. 'One has forgotten to bring me the ice,' she said. When she speaks she gives every syllable its full value, almost as if she were spelling the words. '*On a oublié de m'apporter de la glace.*' She is said to speak Russian, Turkish, Arabic, Dutch and German as well as French – an exotic list which reflects elements of her birth and early youth. We talked of 'art', 'literature' and 'music'; at least the others talked. I can never think what to say about such things, and so focused my attention on the noises of the *riad* beyond the coloured light that flowed from the lantern. I could hear birds truculently unable to sleep, and the rustling of little creatures in the vegetation. Where was the house? Perhaps concealed in the deeper shadows cast by the encircling walls of the *riad*. And where was Mademoiselle de V.'s mother? Of her mother I knew only that she was over eighty and had been a great beauty. Was she concealed in a house itself concealed? Possibly because I was silent, Mademoiselle de V. thought that I was bored, though I was not. 'Would you like to see?' she asked me. She had risen from her stool.

She unhooked the lantern. It was not the house and her '*petit musée*' that we were going to see. '*Nous allons faire le tour de la propriété,*' she told the others and we left them to their discussion in pitch darkness. They did not seem at all surprised. Maurice D—'s voice came after us as Mademoiselle de V. walked away in her aura of lantern-light with me following: '*Comment cela s'expliquet-il, selon vous* . . . ?' he was asking someone. Maurice D— will listen patiently and is then apt to have the last word, *selon lui*. Their voices were slowly smothered by the darkness and we did not even hear the problem posed.

There is a safety in lantern-light that is absent from that of an electric torch. Perhaps it is because a lantern throws its protective beam in a full circle, whereas a torch concentrates itself into a cone, leaving you vulnerable through three hundred degrees of shadowy ambush.

'*Tout d'abord la poule bressane,*' Mademoiselle de V. was announcing.

'*Et la dinde?*'

'Of course! Both. They nest together.'

They were sleeping, these two creatures of Destiny, behind their heap of stones at the far end of the *riad*. I had pictured them lit by the sun, flashing, lively beauties and jewelled with colour. Moreover, I had not been told that the country-cockerel (the one which has transferred his affections from the *poule paralysée* to the well-born newcomer) has taken to roosting in the neck-feathers of the turkey-hen. This, however, is the case. He seemed very comfortable.

'*N'est-ce pas, que c'est gentil?*'

'Very *gentil.*' But I was thinking of the poor barn-door paralytic and Mademoiselle de V. must have divined this for she went on: '*L'affligée ne vient jamais jusqu'à ce coin.*'

'She sleeps alone, the afflicted one?' I asked.

Why did she not come as far as this corner? I wanted to know. Was it fear? Hatred? Prison bars?

'Quite alone.' Mademoiselle de V. poked at the *poule bressane* so that she should bestir herself and enable me to see her better. She was almost hidden by the turkey-hen. A head and a beady eye flickered up at us, and I admired her. I also said something complimentary about the turkey-hen.

'She has four eggs and the turkey-hen has two,' Mademoiselle de V. said proudly. 'It will be very soon now.'

We left them clucking softly to each other. The cockerel had not even awoken.

Pigeons and cats were everywhere; the pigeons in groups, trying to sleep, some in a palm tree, others in baskets like rat-traps suspended against a wall. The cats crouched singly, beneath a *laurier-rose*, behind a *jarre*, one of them in a niche over the entrance-vestibule. Other cats were lurking where the beam of the lantern could hardly reach them.

'That is Daisy.' She pronounced the name *Da–ee–zee*. 'Da–ee–zee is very *sensible* to the *consonance* "*ssss–uh!*" ' This *consonance*, I learnt, causes Daisy to leap on to your shoulder and rub herself against your neck. 'It is curious, is it not?' she asked. I agreed.

'The *consonance* "*ssss–uh*" – what can it signify? Do you know, monsieur?'

I laughed and said that I did not know, but my laugh distressed Mademoiselle de V. Or can it be that she was laughing at me? She said she felt sure that I knew what it meant but that I did not care to say. Did it perhaps have some meaning . . . well, *plutôt déplaisant, grossier* – vulgar? I begged her to believe that I did not know at all but felt bound to ask how they had discovered this *consonance* and its effect on Daisy. She could not remember. Someone had said it by chance one day, and since then she would say it occasionally in order to keep Daisy in good humour. She then told me more about the cats, of which, at the moment, there appear to be seven. They all stem from a patriarch called Titan who has since disappeared magically, or at least definitively. Titan first coupled himself with Daisy – by some accident of the moon and human carelessness – and later with one or other of their progeny. 'And now the little brothers and sisters are all at the same time cousins and aunts,' she went on, stating a simple fact of nature, 'like the Pharaohs.'

' "*Ssss–uh!*" ' I said, but it was not Daisy after all. I followed Mademoiselle de V. across the *riad*, the palm fronds lashing back into my face.

We were approaching a little decorated pavilion. I knew what to expect now.

'*L'affligée*,' murmured Mademoiselle de V. She was kneeling close to a broken wooden lattice. In the shadows I could see that she was smiling sadly. Then she stretched her hand through a breach in the lattice-work and routed about. There was an angry squawking and the sound of wings, but she did not flinch. She withdrew her hand. There was an egg in it.

'*Regardez, monsieur*,' she said. 'Every day. And always these soft shells.'

'Perhaps she needs grit.'

'There is grit everywhere for the taking,' she replied morosely, swinging the lantern round. 'She has only to come out and take it. But she never comes out now. No. It has some other meaning.'

'She could come out if she wanted to, couldn't she?' I said. 'Can I at least see her?'

'Yes. If you do not disturb her. Look!'

For a moment she held the lantern close to the wooden lattice and I had a glimpse of a beak and two eyes black as the night that surrounded them, and filled with malice.

'*La pauvre . . .*' Mademoiselle de V. rose to her feet again.

Had she not seen the look, then?

When we returned to the circle Maurice D— said to me: 'Mayne, *selon vous*, what is the real domain of literature, as compared with that of poetry?'

'You know perfectly well that you deny me the slightest feeling for poetry,' I told him. 'Why ask me?'

'That is why,' he said.

And that is why I refused to answer, though I could perfectly well have made up some reply.

The moon was rising. The sky which had hitherto been indistinguishable from the blackness of the walls now floated above us, a rectangle of milky fluorescence, clouded, starless, dividing our world from infinity. The cocktail was finished. There was a squawk in the remote darkness, and I thought I recognized the voice. But Mademoiselle de V. took no notice. She behaved as if the servants were disputing too loudly behind the green-baize doors that blanket them from the *beau monde* gathered round her table. '*Une tartine, madame?*' she suggested, handing a plate to one of her guests.

* * *

'Why did you not answer my greetings?' Idrees the *simsar* demanded as he came on to the café terrace. '*Je te salue et tu fais comme si tu n'as rien vu! Qu'est-ce que c'est que cette saloperie, hein?*' Idrees always speaks French with me. As a matter of fact, I had seen him approaching with his two friends and I had pretended not to, because I wanted to finish a passage I was working on.

'But I didn't see you, Idrees. I'm so sorry.'

'Oh yes, you did see! I saw! It was impolite not to answer my greeting.'

I capitulated and admitted my fault. 'You see, I was in the middle of something – I still am; and I thought that if once we started on the "*lā-bās-'aleyk's*" and the "*hatta-enta-lā-bās's*" I would forget what I was intending to write.'

'It is rude,' he repeated.

'And it is rude to stand there without introducing me to your friend, Idrees. I know Moulay Yacoub – but . . . '

'Oh! Oh, yes. This is Sidi Haroon bin Ahmed.' We went through the how-d'you-dos and they all sat down at my table. I turned to Idrees again.

'You understand, Idrees, all this greeting takes so long, and I was busy, and anyway you only wanted to pass the time of day, so I pretended not to have seen you.'

'Very rude for a Muslim,' he said. 'If you were a Muslim . . . '

'But *you* do it. I've seen you.'

He considered this for a moment and said, 'When I am passing on my bicycle it is not the same. But now . . . '

'Well? What is the difference?'

'The difference is that I wished to say something to you. Something much to your benefit. Probably now I shall not say it.'

Si Haroon-Sidi or Si – it's the same thing – had been following the conversation with a little difficulty, but he knew that Idrees had scored a point and so supported him with nods.

'How could *I* know that you had something to tell me?' I asked Idrees.

He ignored the question and said, 'Yet I *shall* say it, because you are a *berrāni* and do not fully understand yet. *Eh bien*, we – me and Moulay Yacoub and Sidi Haroon and you – are intending to go to the Aguedal for a feast, *Insha' Allah*. It will be cool there. Water, trees.'

The Aguedal is a huge, walled-in orchard, certainly two miles long or more and about a mile wide, at the southern extremity of the city. It was first planted by an Almohade prince in the twelfth century. The greater part is olives, but there are oranges and citrous fruits and two big artificial lakes, and a ruined summer palace. I know all this from observation and the guidebook and have almost reached the point where I regard one particular corner of it as my private property. Naturally enough, the Aguedal is popular for picnics.

'That would be nice,' I said. 'When is it to be?'

'First we will discuss the feast,' Idrees remarked. 'You must know that this is to be a *nzaha b-et-tenzel*, in which everyone gives the money to Sidi Haroon so that he may bring all the food . . . '

Sidi Haroon broke in: ' . . . *l-lham, el-khodra, et-tum, el-ghella, et-tajīn* . . . '

'*Atay, el-garro*,' added Moulay Yacoub. '*Je te prends une cigarette, monsieur, merci beaucoup*.' He helped himself from my pack.

' . . . *et tout cela*,' said Idrees, with a wide gesture. 'You will kindly contribute two hundred francs.'

I said, 'I think I would prefer to *bring* something. When I am invited like this I generally bring chickens, for example.' I was of course thinking of 'Aysha's *dyafa*. As a matter of fact, so far that has been the only occasion that I have been invited like this.

Moulay Yacoub looked surprised. '*Mais c'est une nzaha b-et-tenzel* that is arranged! And it seems to me that you are talking of a *nzaha b-et-frīda*, which is quite different!'

'Oh. How much are *you* contributing, Idrees?'

'Moulay Yacoub is contributing two hundred francs also,' Idrees said, and Moulay Yacoub clutched at his hand and said, 'You are mistaken, my friend. One hundred and fifty. *Tlātīn reál, yak*? It was arranged, Idrees!'

' '*Andek el-haqq, ya Moulay. Tlātīn reál.* And for you, Monsieur Peter, *deux cents francs*.'

'And you, Idrees?' I asked.

'I? Seventy-five francs, because I am poorer. Sidi Haroon is not giving any money because he has none. But he is a good cook, so that he will contribute his skill in cooking, *Insha' Allah*.'

'Very well. Let me know when it will be,' I said.

'We do not know when, of course. Soon, *Insha' Allah*. In this hot climate it will be agreeable to make a *nzaha* in the Aguedal. Sidi 'Ali is also to come, so that we may use his *calèche* without payment for going there. The carriage is Sidi 'Ali's contribution.'

We talked of the *nzaha* for a minute or two and then the three of them got up to leave. 'Remember what I have told you about answering the "*lā-bās*" of your friends please, Monsieur Peter,' Idrees said.

I laughed. 'I will take no notice of you if you are on your bicycle, and if you are on your feet I shall *lā-bās* you or I shall not, exactly as I please.'

'What!' he cried, sitting down again and motioning the others to do so too. 'Allow me to explain this to you so that you may not make more mistakes.'

They proceeded to explain. I think that the position is as follows: Of course greetings take a long time, but it is very impolite not to go through with it. If both people should be riding, in *calèches* or on bicycles, it is sometimes enough to make a gesture with the hand and an inclination of the head. If only one is riding, then that person may get out (or off) or not, as he pleases. But if both are on foot and there is no avoiding each other, there is no escape. You should only pretend not to have noticed the other if you can do so effectively. In fact I find it is all exactly as it would be in Europe, except that it takes longer. The trouble is that if one of the two wishes to make an impression, he can hold on to the other person's hand, declining to let go, and run through the whole thing again. All the while he should be looking deep into the other's eyes. It is permissible to pat the other person, if desired.

'And embraces?' I asked them.

Moulay Yacoub laid down the rules. 'It is not generally proper for a Christian to try to embrace a Muslim higher than the hand.'

At this Idrees looked at me, laughed uproariously and slapped Sidi Haroon on the shoulder.

'Just you come to London and try to kiss Christians anywhere!' I said firmly.

'No, no!' cried Idrees, collapsing in helpless laughter on Sidi Haroon's neck. Then he recovered sufficiently to say, 'I was not laughing for Christians, I was laughing for Sidi Haroon,' and he collapsed again. Finally he went on more calmly, 'Because you see, my little Haroon el-Rashid is unable to reach anywhere higher than the hand!' Then they all burst out laughing together, including Sidi Haroon.

I had met Moulay Yacoub before, several times. He is a close friend of Idrees's, a short, plump, likeable man. But this was the first time I had met Sidi Haroon, and the point about him is that he is the tiniest of dwarfs. He is completely unselfconscious about it. The Lord God has wished him to be this size and everyone naturally takes it for granted. Everyone recognizes that occasionally it must be troublesome for him and they help him in various sorts of ways. For example, many give him money for being so small and thus unable to do most of the things which could earn him a salary. If they happen to be passing, victoria-drivers give him lifts from one side of the Djema'a el-Fna to the other, to save his legs. Sidi Haroon did not mind in the least that Idrees should laugh. On the contrary, he was delighted and said, 'And if I am unable to reach the hand I will perhaps bite on the leg!'

They were all rocking with laughter again, and people at the nearby tables came up, begging to be told what it was all about, and they rocked with laughter too when they heard.

Moulay Yacoub was the first to regain his composure. He said that he had an amendment to the rules he had laid down. 'I said wrong. Christians should greet Muslims, of course, but they should *not* attempt the embrace. When the hand-shaking is done, a Christian may lightly kiss the tips of his own fingers, in this way – Bwch! – as if to kiss the fingers honoured by the touch of the other, *ti comprends?*'

'Will you do the same, Moulay Yacoub?'

'And I will do the same.' He had rules for Muslims, now. When a Muslim meets another Muslim superior to himself – like 'Moulays' – he should 'make to kiss the hand'. The shoulder or the neck or the cheek are reserved for other superior persons, or relatives. It would be very improper – and presumptuous – to snatch at a part of the superior person's body that was above the station of the kisser.

So it seems there can be two reasons for withdrawing the hand – or the cheek – from a threatened kiss: either to save the kisser from humbling himself, or to rebuke the kisser for his presumption. I imagine that a look of surprise and distaste distinguishes between the two situations, but apart from this personal comment, the rules come from Moulay Yacoub.

'He's telling you all wrong,' Idrees observed.

'I am telling him correctly. No one kisses you, Idrees,' replied the

Moulay sternly, 'because you are neither Moulay nor beautiful. How should you know anything?'

* * *

The rhythm of life in this city has been changing perceptibly during the past week or two. The atmosphere has become drier and drier, with the thermometer rising. All this time the Sahara has lain patiently beyond the peaks of the Atlas biding its moment, and no one has given a thought to it. But now we remember that we have had no visitors from the desert recently. The caravans have stopped coming. And when we look up we remark that the snows have all melted off the mountains.

'*Quarante degrés*,' the French *boulangère* said to me last week, fanning herself with the *Petit Marocain*. '*On va voir. D'ici une quinzaine, on va voir.*'

People don't move about in the sunshine as they did before, and they go to bed later. The nights have continued cool, however, and it is only in the last three days that I have been leaving the door between my room and the kitchen open, as well as my window, in the hope of creating a draught. The *boulangère* says that most of the European residents of the new town have left for France or the Atlantic coast – those that can afford to. The Djema'a el-Fna is half-empty from about midday till six o'clock, and the cafés lower their canvas blinds so that it is no longer pleasant to sit on the terrace of the Café de France and write. I work at home on the suitcase as best I can. But when evening comes, it is heavenly (or appears to be), and I have taken to strolling about on the Djema'a el-Fna after dinner, often in the company of Maurice D—. We have a coffee together and then stroll, up and down, up and down, talking. Sometimes he tells me about China and Indo-China and I tell him about places I know, each of us taking pains to show interest in what the other has to say. In actual fact he talks well, and I am glad to listen. I then make him listen to me.

He is a curious man. Intellectually, he is purely French, and of a high order at that – but temperamentally he is Oriental. He has told me how he came here a year or more ago for a visit, and how within a couple of weeks he had bought a house in the knowledge that it was here that he must settle. He asked me why I came, and I prevaricated: it seemed presumptuous to have chosen Marrakesh with a pin, blindfold, and then to have found that I was entirely happy with my choice. But I know why he chose it. There is something Mongol about it to which he can respond immediately. I asked him about this. I was thinking about the pavilion, partly, but more about the *Mechouar* beyond the Sultan's palace. The Sultan has a palace in Marrakesh and outside its battlements lie two enormous, flat, empty *places*. They are surrounded by walls of their own, divided from each other by a common wall pierced with an arch. It is here that the Sultan shows himself to the people when he visits the city, and they are called *Mechouar*. I am drawn by their emptiness, and each time I go to the Aguedal, which involves passing through them, their Mongol aspects strike me – China of the far north, I say to myself. At intervals along the walls are little gates, or watch-houses, surmounted by roofs of green tiling which suggest pagodas. But it is coarser than anything I think of as purely Chinese. And in the same way there is often something suggestively Mongol about the features of Berbers, but again coarser, heavier. Maurice D— who is so very Mongolian in looks has yet sometimes been asked if he is a Moor, or at least a Muslim from some other country. So Moors can see it too, and yet, as far as I know, the races have no common ancestry of any kind, and I have never heard this Mongol aspect commented upon, or read of it. Maurice admitted it readily when I asked him.

'I feel at peace here,' he said. 'I think I understand the people, and that perhaps they understand me.'

It is only now that I begin to understand him.

* * *

The air we breathe has changed suddenly to an eddying whirligig of heat, laden with grit. Men hide their faces in the hoods of their *djellabas* and remember the Sahara now. Of course, things have been working up for some days. There has been a greyness in the skies over the Atlas and we seem to have been living in a little microcosm of sunshine while something banked itself up behind us. The *Sherghi*. It has been filling its lungs with the sands of the Sahara, gathering itself together while we waited a little apprehensively, and now at last it has attacked. It is appalling – related to the *scirocco* but infinitely less civilized. This is what the people of Tangier meant when they said that I was mad to come to Marrakesh in the summer, and they have been wrong until now. Mercifully the *Sherghi* is said to respond to the magic of numbers, and works to a formula 3 – 3 – 3. The numbers represent days and, at intervals of three, some power decides whether the *Sherghi* should continue for a further three – and then a further three. This is the first day of the first three, and I think I prefer to remain stifled at home, with what I can find to eat in the biscuit tin I use as a store-cupboard, rather than brave the *Sherghi* and discover that perhaps all the stalls in the market are closed because the stall-holders have been less brave. The *Sherghi* is intolerable.

* * *

The *boulangère* made a mockery of a smile and said, '*Quarante-quatre hier, et quarante-cinq avant-hier*. The first day was only forty-two.'

Her sensibilities are evidently finer than my own. I am unable to distinguish between forty-two degrees and forty-five, as well as unable to convert Centigrade readings to Fahrenheit. I am only able to say that I thank God for having ordered the *Sherghi* to dissolve itself after the first period of three. My skin has a film over it, but the sun is shining again as if it had never stopped doing so, and people smile like men rescued from a train-smash – tentative, uncertain of themselves. Everyone looks very grubby, so the *hammāms* will be full tonight.

* * *

The *Sherghi* has unexpectedly revived and is worse than ever. As it must now continue for its second period of three and, for all we know, for a third period also, Maurice D— and I have decided to leave these inland plains for the Atlantic. It is only two hours by autocar to Safi and we leave at dawn.

'*Nous ferons du camping*,' said Maurice D—. '*Je m'occupe de tous les arrangements. Alors*, let us make a list . . . '

Derb esh-Shems (3)

THE THRUST OF THE WAVES and their long, sighing withdrawal makes a *thrrump* and a *wheeesh* in the darkness ahead of us. I write by the gleam of a little nineteenth-century paraffin lamp that forms part of Maurice's camping equipment. It is called '*la lampe Pigeon*'. It is really a night-light for Second-Empire nurseries – of graceful design, brass, with a calligraphic inscription. It has a glass shade which fits into a crown of metal, pierced with a pattern of *fleurs-de-lys*. The spindle which was intended for winding the wick up and down so long ago does so no longer. Tonight Maurice has a safety-pin for this. '*La lampe Pigeon*' gives a tiny yellow light that has scarcely flickered at all since the wind dropped. It illumines our restricted world – in particular Maurice (who looks more Chinese than ever, with no clothes except a yard of batik), the undersides of the rock, and me. I am dressed in tartan drawers.

We have brought a tent with us – a tent so light and convenient that it will roll up and contain itself in something not much larger than a large sponge-bag. It is made of nylon, sides and groundsheet all in one. But the sand on this beach is as soft as a feather bed, offering no hold for tent-pegs – at least this was the case at sundown – when the wind came whipping over the sea, filling the gossamer envelope of the tent as we tried to pitch it, flicking the pegs out as fast as we could bang them in.

Actually, Maurice banged them in while I lay inside the tent, spread-eagled to hold its corners in position with my hands and feet. Lying inside this mad, prancing, runaway balloon of a tent, I soon had so strong an impression that the wind was in my own stomach that I had to come out.

We were unable to pitch the thing and have therefore decided that we shall do as well in a crevice between two large overhanging rocks, the tent folded to serve as a groundsheet. It is this crevice that '*la lampe Pigeon*' now lights with its little yellow gleam. The wind has dropped, but it may be lurking somewhere, and it is too dark to think of tents again. And why should we? We are quite resigned, and it is getting less oppressive as night advances. The heat has been appalling all day, and they were saying in the little seaport town of Safi when we started out to look for a campsite that no living person can remember it hotter. That was this morning, before *déjeuner*. It is night now and the moon will soon be up.

Maurice says it is very poetic. '*Le site est plein de poésie*,' he says, and he is right. The little bay with its two protective promontories, the smooth yellow of the sands, the cliffs towering behind us in striations of mustard and a shot-mauve-and-steel like taffeta – these strange colours that we remember from an hour or two ago but can see no longer because they have been swallowed up in the purple of the night. The site is full of *poésie*. Quite close to us a cascade of greenery tumbles down the cliffs and halts suddenly at a point perhaps fifty foot above the beach. It must mean water, fresh water. We shall explore in the morning. It is too dark now. We shan't bother about supper; we are not hungry. I am nevertheless exceedingly thirsty – all that trudging and site-searching, laden with rucksacks, with the *batterie de cuisine*, with our *matelas pneumatiques*, with Maurice's two-volume edition of Spengler's *Declin de l'Occident* and three-volume edition of Malraux's *Psychologie de l'Art*, and some Edward Lear for me, with the elaborate American War Department Disposals paraffin-vapour cooker, not to mention the weight of the provisions and the cruel heat of the sun. I would like to have some coffee at least, but Maurice has just said; with an impassive Chinese face, that coffee prevents slumber. It is obvious that he doesn't wish to search for the stove which is somewhere in the shadows behind us. He knows my prejudice against paraffin-vapour stoves will prevent me from lighting it even if I can find it. I shall perhaps make do with *vin rosé*, warm and undrinkable, or water. Maurice has foreseen everything. 'We must preserve the water, in case . . . ,' he says. I know what he means, though neither of us has yet admitted that the spring of fresh water may be foul. Neither will admit this until the facts spring into the open like jungle tigers. We have of course ignored the first rule of *le camping*: to make sure of the water supply. Never mind. There is nothing to be done about it now. We cannot escape from this enclosed and beautiful bay tonight. Tomorrow will be time enough to consider such problems. At present we are hoping to sleep.

'*C'est comme ça, le camping*,' Maurice is telling me as if it will be of some comfort. '*Un mélange de délices et d'ennuis* . . . ' The moon is coming up now. In two days it will be full. We are fatigued – a good, healthy, physical fatigue, naturally. Maurice has tied a handkerchief over his eyes and settled down to rest.

* * *

A new day. No doubt it will be hot later, but for the moment it is cool and delicious. I have been looking out of the rock crevice and am delighted to find that the bay is as beautiful as we have been saying so determinedly. The sun has risen behind the cliffs so that the sand is still in shadow but the waves, where they break, are touched with brilliance, a long moving crescent of brilliance. There is a scalloping of sea-wrack and little pieces of what seems to be charcoal marking the point where the tide has reached during the night and, by a curious chance, our rocks stand midway between two swags of this uneven high-water line. Though we slept well, there was a period when the wind drove veils of sand into the rock crevice and later, about one o'clock, when for an hour we believed ourselves threatened by the sea. We sat up, waiting to be drowned and too tired to protest, but the waves went back again. During that hour, I had time to learn that a pneumatic mattress just sufficiently inflated to support the distributed weight of a body at full length is insufficiently inflated to support the same body balanced on its rump. Sitting, it was as if I were sitting on whatever was underneath the mattress – in this case, rock. We slept again when the tide went back. Now, in the cool of the morning, we have already made and eaten our breakfast – coffee, porridge (which Maurice calls 'Quakaire'), bread and butter, glistening with sand granules. The American stove, fearlessly operated by Maurice, has worked like magic. 'Quakaire' uses up a lot of water, and our emergency supplies are almost gone. In a minute I shall attempt to scale the cliff-face, armed with a canvas bucket, and get at that spring.

* * *

I have scaled the cliff-face. Fifty foot above the beach where the tumbling line of greenery suddenly stops, there proved to be a shelf, hidden by the bamboos which grow round the edge of it. In the middle of the shelf is a pool which fills slowly with water that comes trickling down from above. Someone had stuck a section of bamboo leaf into the clayey substance of the cliff, in such a manner that water flows along the leaf and spills over the point of it in a pipette-thin stream. A foot or so below the leaf the same person had also stuck a couple of bamboo twigs horizontally into the clay as a support for his rusty mug. This was someone who had reached the shelf before me. He was an old Moor, and he must have been there for some little while because already he had had time to wash out a ragged-looking coat of military cut, a shirt and a patchwork *djellaba*. These garments were hanging out to dry amongst the bamboos. He was now starting on his pantaloons. He had wetted them and laid them on a stone bordering the pool and was rhythmically stamping some of the dirt out of them. For soap he used a fleshy-looking plant that I had seen growing at the foot of the cliff. With each stamp he blew through his teeth, and he was as naked as a fish except for his turban. He greeted me very politely, all the same, and at once removed his mug so that I might fill our bucket. I have not actually managed to fill it because it would take too long and, moreover, I could see from the first inch that the water drawn from the leaf was almost as foul as the water in which the old man was washing his pantaloons. We exchanged details of personal history (he is an old soldier, for example, *Classe* 1914) and he said that the water was good to drink but should be passed through a cloth to filter off the impurities. 'Thus,' he said, demonstrating with the tail of his turban. He had finished the pantaloons and begun on a tiny *djellaba* by now.

'Thank you,' I said, and then pointed to the *djellaba*. 'Your son's?'

'No.' He sighed, and looked down at the wrinkled ravages of time, adding bitterly, 'My wife is no good.'

I told him how sorry I was and he said that that was the way God had willed it and it was a bit late now.

'Nonsense,' I exclaimed. 'Look at Abraham!'

'Ibrahim was a prophet,' he said with resignation, and returned to the question of water. 'It is good from the leaf. You can see. Look! Of course I am obliged to wash my turban in any case.'

A thickish red deposit now stained the turban-tail. Strange. I had not expected it to be so red. Maurice believes that boiling removes all impurities from water. He adds that in boiling water for tea the Chinese rule is that the water bubbles should not exceed the size of shrimps' eyes. But, looking at this water, I was not sure if shrimps' eyes would prove to be big enough.

I thanked the old man, and clambered down to the beach again with the bucket. I was thinking, 'If we filter it and leave it standing, filter it again, boil and reboil, perhaps by lunchtime . . . '

We lazed in the sun and bathed. The sea was ice-cold. When the day grew hotter, we lazed in the shadow of our rocks and bathed again. A party of Moorish women appeared, picking their way round the promontory. They seemed elaborately dressed for beach-strollers and, as they came nearer, we could see that none except the biggest, whose gait suggested an old woman, wore a veil. They seemed not to notice us as they settled themselves down twenty yards away and undressed. It was a confusing performance. They had so many garments, all shapeless, so many bits and pieces, so many belts and clips and etceteras. One of the girls proved to be wearing a brassière and nylon panties under all her finery, and a good many bracelets – gold. The other two young ones just wrapped a length of cloth round their hips leaving their breasts bare – big, swelling, Gauguin breasts. They all gave their clothes to the old woman who sat guarding them. If the girls had been European I would have put their ages at between twenty and twenty-five; Moors, they were probably a good deal younger.

Then they bathed. They ran, the three of them, to the edge of the sea, hand in hand, squeaking, tossed their heads, turned, slapped each other playfully, scampered back, pretended to trip, actually fell, were slightly wetted by a wave, screamed again and were wetted again, clung together for protection and did not so much as glance our way except to make sure that we were watching. Of course we were watching. I looked at Maurice.

'Are they whores or little carefree virgins?'

'They are little virgins,' he said. 'And that must be their nurse.' He said 'nurse' in English, pronouncing it as if it were spelt *neeurse.*

I agreed. 'They are little Gauguin virgins.'

Then suddenly the nurse started screaming. The girls glanced round with the most convincing anxiety and saw for the first time, as indeed did we, two shaven Moorish heads peering from behind a rock – shaven heads and moustaches. The three girls promptly closed into a circle, their arms round each other's necks, and knelt quite silent in the surf. Someone's left breast was peeping out from under her arm but it was quickly thumbed back into hiding. Three fuzzy heads, three backs, three square behinds. One of the shaven-heads whistled. The girls quivered, screamed in unison (who knew which of them had been marked by Fate, after all?); the Moors laughed and the nurse came shrieking as fast as her legs could carry her to throw a *hāik*, as a fisherman casts his net, over all that shrinking flesh. Now only the three behinds were visible. It was a very moving spectacle. Meantime, another Moor had come up, rather grand in a *djellaba* with a poignard slung under his left armpit. I cannot imagine where he had come from. He said something to the old woman which impressed her. Then he waved to the shaven heads who hid themselves behind their rock again. To us he gave a cold, warning glance and stalked away. The old woman collected her charges' clothes and they all waddled off down the beach. We saw the grand Moor speak to them again and a wrangle ensue, but the man won. The girls' spirits were broken, evidently.

'Do you think they aren't virgins after all?' I suggested to Maurice. 'And that the man is the one who collects the takings?'

We could only guess at the truth. Nor did the final episode reveal it to us. Furtively, the girls came back and addressed us through the layers of clothing and veils and belts they had again assumed. The grand Moor had gone – or if he had not altogether gone, he was in hiding. They told us that he claimed to be an official, a policeman, and had said to them, '*Défendu!*' What was forbidden? None of us knew.

'I think it may be forbidden to show your breasts and behinds on the beach,' I said in Arabic as accurately as I could.

They shrieked with horror. 'Never, never!' they wailed. 'Not I!'

'*You* did,' I said, pointing, 'and *you*. And the third girl's wet drawers did nothing to help. It was very shameful.'

'Never, never,' they wailed, and one added, jingling her bracelets, 'The child of devils! He desired my gold.' Her eyes flashed fire. 'Yes. He demanded my gold.'

What can the truth have been?

The shaven-heads sat watching from their rock. They looked quite pleased.

'*Yallah!*' the old woman said to her charges, 'Come! Men are animals of ravishment and lust.'

* * *

Before inflating our mattresses last night – the second we have spent in this rock crevice – we built a little wall of sand and sea-smooth stones round the entrance. This was to keep out the sea, and this morning we were gratified to find that it had worked perfectly, in the sense that it had been merely licked with foam and had stood stolid. Moreover, we slept perfectly too. The tide had come up even further than on the previous night, and with considerable energy too, but we owe our deliverance really to the fact that for some reason it had attacked the section of beach in front of us too fiercely to succeed. The force of the waves had driven up a bank of sand they could not surmount. Further along the bay, the comparatively gentle slope has been overrun by the tide to a point much further inshore. We have congratulated ourselves on this. On the other hand, the paraffin-vapour stove does not work any more. So we have had to use twigs and dried bamboo-shoots lying about at the foot of the cliffs.

In my view, though much safer, it is less satisfactory than a stove that works, and it makes a great deal of smoke in the rock crevice. I have decided that the water from the pool is fit only for shaving. This means that we must get drinking water from the town. Safi is two or three kilometres away, but we shall need cigarettes too because some fishermen turned up yesterday afternoon and, seeing a packet lying beside us, asked for some. If the positions had been reversed, and they had owned the packet and we had asked for cigarettes, they would automatically have given us as many as they had. Moors are astonishingly generous in this way. So we have no right to be surprised or annoyed that they left us with but one each.

It is very hot again. If you look up to the cliff-tops you can see the grey veiling of the *Sherghi* flying westwards to drown in the Atlantic. At sundown the *Sherghi* takes a rest, the hot air rises from the poor, parched lands and then the wind from the sea comes roaring in to fill the vacuum. Nature is sometimes very cruel.

By late afternoon I knew that I had had enough of our rock crevice. I had spent most of the day in it because it is really too hot to remain in the sun. Maurice had found a protected section of rock on which he was able to stretch himself out to sleep or read. He appeared quite content. But all our water had gone now. I read a little, tried to write but found that I couldn't concentrate, and put the notebook down again. I bathed, of course, but the sand burns one's feet, and the waters of the Atlantic are cold as a winter douche, and there seems to be no moderation in our present lives. So, at about six, when the cruellest part of the day had passed, I said I would struggle in to the town to get water.

'Don't worry,' I said. 'I will gladly go. Of course it's hot, but that's exactly why we must drink.' I collected our basket, and the paraffin-vapour stove. 'I'll see if I can get this mended. I'll be as quick as I can, but don't wait for me if you get hungry.'

As a matter of fact, I had no intention of returning for supper. I was a little irritated by Maurice's obvious enjoyment of what distressed me. I had even told him that it was all right for the Chinese: God had given them skins which took kindly to grilling, and that it was quite unnecessary for him to lard himself with sunburn lotion. '*J'aime l'odeur*,' he said calmly. I felt that in that case he could perfectly well boil the pool-water for tea, in the Chinese fashion, if he became thirsty before I returned.

It was a walk which would have been delightful but for the pall of heat – over the promontory, across a long beach that has silted up between the promontory and the outermost moles of the harbour. Inside the town it was stifling. I bought bottles of table water called 'Jony', cigarettes, and *thon à l'huile* for breakfast. I also went to the autocar stop and made two reservations in the afternoon coach to Marrakesh for the next day. I had not consulted Maurice about this, but *Sherghi* or no *Sherghi*, three, six or nine, I wish to go home. Then I deposited all my purchases under the sink through the kindness of a *garçon-de-café*, and set out to see the town for the first time. On the day of our arrival we had started off at once on our search for a campsite. This seeing of a new town I like to do alone, of course, because I don't want companions who will tell me things or insist upon asking locals for information. It is an enchanting town, very Portuguese in aspect, and living partly on the bounty of sardines. The sardine shoals which used to swim about off the Portuguese coast have gradually worked their way down to Safi, and show signs of going still further south. In the wake of these shoals are left little ports and canneries that must one day lie idle. Safi has been wise to develop other sources of revenue. In normal circumstances, the town must be alive with people drinking in bars, but not on the evening I spent wandering alone. In fact, I hated my promenade.

I remained in the town for supper, eating at a cheap restaurant, and then sipping a cognac with my coffee on the pavement. I still believed it would get cooler when darkness came. But it did not, and finally when it was quite dark I collected my basket and set off for the rock crevice. It was night by now, though still too early for the moon, and I was annoyed with myself for having slipped away in this unfriendly fashion and not enjoyed it. I was also annoyed with the appalling weight of the 'Jony' bottles.

The track over the promontory, which had seemed so clearly defined by day, was practically unrecognizable under the beam of my torch. From the little *cap*, I could see '*la lampe Pigeon*' as a speck in the distance.

It was certainly getting cooler now, a moist Atlantic coolness I did not care about.

As I made my way along the beach '*la lampe Pigeon*' grew steadily brighter and I suddenly realized that it was shining from some point quite high in the cliff-face, and was probably not '*la lampe Pigeon*' at all. I wondered what had happened. I flashed my torch on and off, vaguely signalling. '*Pigeon*' made no reply. When I drew quite near I discovered Maurice lamp-lit on a platform that stuck out from the cliff. It was quite a climb up to him.

'There was a man who passed,' Maurice said when I had joined him. 'He asked me, "You have the intention to sleep here?", pointing into the grotto. And I replied, "But naturally." '

I turned my torch into the darkness and saw that all our baggage had been transported on to the platform. 'But why all this?' I asked Maurice. I dare say I felt a little guilty and wished to suggest by my tone of voice that he had expended his energies uselessly.

'It is full moon tonight. The man said so. He also said, "The moon will bring the sea into your grotto and destroy you." So I moved the things up. Nice, *n'est-ce pas*?' He was glancing round the platform. 'Do you suppose there will be scorpions?'

I didn't think so, but I was still irritable and so I said, 'Probably,' in a matter-of-fact voice.

Maurice said, 'I have eaten. I did not wait for you, because I knew you wished to pass the evening in the town. I hope you have eaten and that you have enjoyed the promenade.'

* * *

We are back in Marrakesh now. Everyone tells us how lucky we were to have been able to run away and escape the *Sherghi* – which really does seem to have spent itself this time. Of course it is difficult to be sure from conditions observed in the evening, but Maurice, who claims to be sensitive to changes in pressure, says that it will be fine again tomorrow. The sky is clearer, as I can see.

The journey here was abominable. The autocar was crowded, and someone had loaded a sack of fish on the roof which dribbled its juices down the windows and smelt very bad. The heat was still such that the petrol was continually drying up to the point of complete evaporation in the feed, so that the driver had to stop and bind wet rags round it. But we have arrived back, and except for a note, apparently in French, from someone whose signature I cannot clearly read (I suspect it is 'Abdeslem), I am again without worries. The note appears to be a request for a large sum of money, urgent, important. It suggests a rendezvous.

Derb esh-Shems (4)

THE NOTE *is* from 'Abdeslem, though it has obviously been written by someone else for him. It reads:

> Onnui abominable a porte felous cent real sans faute je te prie immediatément je serez place riad larous quatr heure exacte demain inchallah ta camarade fidèle . . .

and then comes that curious signature. But it is 'Abdeslem, I know now. I had supper on the Djema'a el-Fna and afterwards I strolled about for a while with Maurice, and when I finally got home again the night-watchman was sitting beside my door. He engaged me in conversation, first about the *Sherghi* and how, *el-hamdu l-llah*, it seemed to have left us again, then about other matters, and at last about what had been in his mind all the time.

'Your *courrier*? You have found it waiting in the house?'

'But I have all my letters at the *poste restante*.' I did not mention the note which was delivered by hand, without stamps.

'*Ah, oui*. But I think I have seen *courrier* arrive. Is there not something there?' He glanced up at me curiously, and I thought I would test him, in case he knew something. In the neighbourhood they still say that he and 'Abdeslem have been in collusion over the 'new girl' though no one has any proof.

'There is only one little note. But as I cannot read the signature, I shall do nothing about it.'

I saw at once that he was alarmed. 'But you can write – everyone says so! Can you not also read?'

'I can read, but not that signature.'

'It is in French?' (We were speaking in French.) 'I am *ancien militaire*, you know. Do you wish me to read it for you? Moreover not only can I read in French but also write . . . ' And he suddenly stopped as if he had perhaps said too much.

'You can try to read it if you like. I should be very much obliged to you.'

I fetched the note, and we lit a match to read it by. The night-watchman read the signature without the least difficulty. He also proceeded to read the text, which I have no doubt he wrote himself.

'What do you think it means?' I asked him.

'*Eh bien. "Onnui abominable"*. That is clear. It is as it says, *ennui abominable. Le pauvre* 'Abdeslem is in great trouble. And then that money is required, which is very clear too. Five hundred francs – that is the *felūs cent reál.* Immediate. And then the meeting. You know Riad l-'Arous? It is not far. *Ce n'est qu'à deux cents mètres d'ici.*'

'I have very little money, you know. I don't think I . . . '

' . . . for your *friend*? Your *camarade fidèle* – look, it is all written here in the note – *ta camarade fidèle* 'Abdeslem! Oh, monsieur, this would be a *hashouma* beyond everything!' A *hashouma* is a disgrace, evidently in this case the sort of shame that comes down upon a man who fails in his duty. 'At four tomorrow. That is all. Ah, it is the easiest little affair in the world! It is as *nothing*, what he asks of his dearest friend!'

'Well, we shall see. Perhaps.'

'*Tu jures . . . ?*'

'No. I make no promises, but I will think about it.'

'You will not consult 'Aysha, *naturellement.*'

'No.'

'*C'est de la sorcellerie, j'en suis sûr.*'

I went to the rendezvous with five hundred francs in my pocket and

'Abdeslem was half an hour late, looking like a poor old man who had lost hope.

'Well, what is it, 'Abdeslem?' I asked.

Briefly, he has been bewitched; by a woman associate of 'Aysha's who supplied the particular powders and, more especially, the spells. His head is turning round and round inside. The 'new girl' has been bewitched too, but in a different manner, by the same person and at 'Aysha's request. 'Abdeslem is in grave need. It will cost money. He has therefore called upon his dearest and most faithful friend – me – to assist in the matter. I did not argue about this.

'It is a strange matter, Monsieur Raoul,' he said.

'I am not Monsieur Roaul, but Monsieur Peter.' I wondered who Monsieur Roaul could be.

'You are right. Monsieur Raoul is another gentleman. I met him once and gave him my photograph. I also received a postcard from this gentleman. Would you like to see? I have it here.'

'I don't want you to bother.'

'It is no bother-*shī bās mā kāin*.'

I caught at him by the arm as he fumbled for his *portefeuille*. 'Listen, 'Abdeslem. There are other, bigger bothers to attend to. If you want me to help, you must tell me exactly what the *ennui* is.'

'Ah, *that* . . .' and he suddenly deflated again, once more becoming an old man burdened with intolerable cares. '*Une sorcière*,' he whispered darkly. 'And then there is 'Aysha. You heard what she did?'

'I heard. How did you get out?'

'Some day I will tell. But today I tell you of other matters. *L-'ayn! Darbetni l-'ayn el-qbiha*! It is the evil eye!'

'Whose?' I believe it is important to know this.

'*Mā n'aref*! I don't know! But it is *excessivement mauvais*. O Monsieur Peter, *je souffre, je souffre, comme je souffre*! God alone can help me, God is greatest! And you can give the money, please. Five hundred francs.'

'But for what purpose is this money, 'Abdeslem? I must know.'

He was rapidly unbuttoning the collar of his shirt, and now produced a little tin amulet attached to a cord. 'You see this? Two hundred francs, and no good at all! And this?' He thrust out his arm so that the shirt-cuff slipped back a few inches, revealing a piece of thread with a bobble on it. '*Egalement*! But, by the grace of God, cheaper a little. But now there is a lady,' he went on in a very confidential voice, 'who is able to give me something which will not only take off the evil, but also put it back where it comes from with pains like those of fire. Five hundred francs . . . no, no, please wait, Monsieur Peter, wait, please! Listen, it is a double matter – as if it were *deux sorcelleries*, each only two hundred and fifty francs! You understand? To take from *here* . . . and to put *here* . . . '

'And that girl? That very pretty girl who came to 'Aysha's *dyafa*? What about her?'

'That girl has already been cured of the evil spells. A man who had money – a gentleman in the police, I think – was able to arrange it. But, alas, there is no man with *felūs* for me, and I am therefore compelled to suffer alone, my friends *zertiyīn*, my . . . '

'*Zertiyīn? What* about your friends? I have not heard this word.'

'*Zerti* is he who flees, the *harāmi*.'

'I see. But I would like to know more, before I can give money. Take me please to the lady who says she can help if you pay.'

'She will not like because you are *Nasrāni*.'

'In that case – '

' . . . but if you wish,' he said hurriedly, 'I will ask her. I will say this is *spécial*. Give me one hundred francs now and tomorrow come again and we shall see.'

'I will come again, *Insha' Allah*, directly you can tell me that everything is arranged and that I may be present at the unbewitchment.'

He looked very sombre as he turned towards me. 'And if the evil completes itself before that day?'

'If it kills you, you mean? Do you think it will?'

'It will be your fault. The death of a Muslim will be on your head, Monsieur Peter.'

'You can take me to the lady now, if you like.'

'Now? This is a matter for the night hours and it is only four o'clock!'

'Then name the night.'

'I will come soon and name it.' He started to roll his eyes and wail, '*Ya willi! Ana mekshūf! Ya willi, willi, willi, willi . . .*'

* * *

'Aysha was round this morning with a new scheme. She knows that I do my own cooking, such as it is, because she sees me come back from the market with my purchases, and she naturally assumes that I like Moorish food.

'Does it please you, *faire la cuisine?*' she asked me, and I said that while I liked the idea of cooking, I didn't like doing it, particularly in my 'kitchen' which is even less than a platform at the top of the stairs.

'I do it very badly,' I admitted, 'And moreover it takes too much of the morning.'

'Ah,' she said. 'And if perhaps I prepare the *déjeuner* for you? That would please you?'

It would, as a matter of fact. I don't think I have anything to fear from 'Aysha. I don't set her heart beating, and she knows perfectly well that even if I were magicked into desiring her, there would be no money in it. Therefore it seemed to me a very sensible proposal. It is obvious that two people can feed for very much less than twice the cost of one, so we should both save on it; at least she would.

'Yes. It would please me. What would you charge your *pensionnaire*, 'Aysha? Just *déjeuner*, nothing else.'

'I will make the *calcul*,' she said and then suddenly, as if to trap me, 'How is 'Abdeslem?'

''Abdeslem?' I didn't know she knew I had seen him yesterday. How quickly news travels in this city! 'He has his *ennuis*, it seems.' I paused, thought for a moment and then looked squarely at her. ''Aysha! What did you and your friend do to him?'

'*Rien*. I told you. Just simply the possets. To cool him.'

'No. More than that.'

'Very little more. A something particular, a powder, to put him to rest for a while, *peut-être*.'

'More. Something else too.'

'*Rien*.' She waved to a passing neighbour and tried to lure him into a conversation, but the man was in a hurry and pretended not to see her. I caught 'Aysha by the shoulder and turned her about so that I could look her in the eyes.

'Something more too, 'Aysha! At least the other did something more, at your request. Isn't that true?'

She stood silent, biting her tongue. Then she released it and said, ''Abdeslem is unworthy to be thought about.'

'You know that the . . . the girl who came to your *dyafa* is released?'

'Zwina? *La fiancée de Si Fulan?* Ah, the trouble that you cause me, Monsieur Peter! That poor beautiful girl . . .

'Exactly. I speak not of *la fiancée* but of that beautiful girl, the other. You have heard that she is long ago released from the wishes that were put upon her?'

She spat. 'She is only a *putain* who has been given a lesson and has learnt it. And in any case the lady who . . . who did what she did to teach 'Abdeslem has long departed for her *bled*. I do not even know her name. She is a lady unknown to me entirely.'

But 'Aysha was wavering, so I pressed on with my advantage, rather pleased with myself. 'Of course I admit it is important for the person bewitched to know the identity of the person bewitching. That is clear. But supposing 'Abdeslem believed it was you yourself, 'Aysha? Naturally it is impossible, but bewitched persons have heads receptive to belief. In that case, and supposing you were kind enough to remove the magic with – oh, I don't know what exactly, but perhaps by stirring the *couscous* with an olive branch instead of with a dead-man's-hand, for example (we could find out about that, I am sure) – then might he not be both grateful and eternally loving? You think it is a good idea?'

For a brief moment, she stared down the alley in thought. Then she said, 'I fear it is too late for him to be *sincèrement* loving, Monsieur Peter, because of those possets.'

'Don't start making difficulties at this stage, please, because I am sure that *something* could be done. If you don't know, then *renseigne-toi!* There are ladies in the city who do know. Inform yourself quickly before it is too late, 'Aysha!'

Frowning, she passed her hand over her forehead, 'For your sake perhaps, Monsieur Peter, but not for 'Abdeslem's, I will consider the matter. I will inform myself.' She even managed a watery smile, and then suddenly it collapsed. 'But it will be *Ramadan* in a day or two! We must wait till the moon of *Shuwwāl*!'

'Is *Shuwwāl* the moon after *Ramadan?* But why not *Ramadan?* It is a good, worthy thing you would be attempting! Not a bad! It is, I am sure, a very suitable matter for the *Ramadan* moon. It is nothing more nor less than the bringing back of a man to his loved one!'

'*Je me demande si . . .*'

'I congratulate you on your decision, 'Aysha.'

* * *

I suddenly realize that the new moon is not due for nearly a fortnight. I must remind 'Aysha of this in the hope that she will 'inform herself' as quickly as possible, if she really does not know how to release 'Abdeslem from his *ennuis*. I must also get in touch with 'Abdeslem somehow. Possibly the night-watchman will know where he is to be found, though he pretends not to.

* * *

Everyone concerned is being exceedingly unco-operative. 'Aysha says that she hasn't discovered the formula yet, and the night-watchman still pretends not to know where 'Abdeslem is (though I am sure he must have been in touch with him). And finally, of course, 'Abdeslem has failed to get in touch with me himself. Ten days have passed, and *Ramadan* begins very soon now.

Oh well, why should I bother? Except that I am committed more or less to paying for 'Abdeslem's chosen *sorcière* if I cannot bring him and 'Aysha together as planned.

I shall let things slide . . .

* * *

Ramadan started with the new moon – a little pine-nut of a moon which followed the sun down over the horizon so rapidly that it scarcely counted, except to inaugurate the month of fasting. From dawn – from the moment it becomes possible to distinguish between a white thread and a black – to the setting of the sun, a complete fast is required of all Muslims who have reached the age of puberty. Nearly everyone is strictly observing it. At this season – high summer – it must be hard to bear. The *Sherghi* is safely behind us (though it may come again) but the thermometer still registers in the forty-threes and -fours: dry, blazing, a heavy load. It is so hot that you do not even seem to sweat. The moisture dries at once, and your shirt feels brittle as paper. For sixteen hours of the twenty-four, for the twenty-eight days of the moon's cycle, Muslims may neither eat nor drink nor smoke – and in theory, which often approaches practice, must exclude all evil or unworthy thoughts from their heads. Tempers run high towards evening under this strain. People who are preparing to fight each other in the streets have to be continually soothed and separated.

Some people – Idrees the *simsar*, for example – simply don't leave home all day. He says he finds it easier to bear if he is asleep. Less fortunate people have to continue working in the ordinary way. Moreover, when 'Aysha suggested over a fortnight ago that she should provide me with *déjeuner*, she had forgotten that she would be unable to eat *déjeuner* herself during *Ramadan*, so the plan has had to be sidetracked. Perhaps we shall return to it later.

I have been asked several times if I am keeping the fast; obviously because the existence of blacklegs like myself in the *derb* is infuriating. The only thing that makes the discipline of the fast endurable for the Marrakeshis is the fact that it is a communal martyrdom. I avoid smoking in the streets during the forbidden hours, or drinking where others can see me.

Idrees's plump friend, Moulay Yacoub, expects to have lost five or six kilos by the time the fast ends. 'You will see,' he remarked complacently, sucking his fat cheeks in to show how he will look. But Idrees himself is more worried about not being able to smoke.

'Do you know, Monsieur Peter, that even if someone else's smoking got inside my nose, my fast would be spoiled?'

'But you are allowed to wash your mouth out with water, aren't you?'

'Of course – and you spit the water away again: you *must* spit it away!

And how can you spit the smoke if it gets in? If my fast is spoiled, I have to fast an extra day for each spoiling.'

'I am as dry as a little dead leaf,' Moulay Yacoub informed us. 'Therefore I sit motionless with my feet in a big bucket of water.'

'And when they blow the trumpets – you have heard the trumpets? – and the gun fires like just now, I am so exhausted with fasting that I am almost unable to drink the *harira*.' This was Idrees again, but the Moulay broke in, 'If *you* were fasting, Monsieur Peter, you might often come to my house for the *harira*. The *harira* at my house is better than this.'

'*Harira?*'

'This! The breakfasting soup, of course! Very excellent at my house. But you are not fasting.'

They were both very pleased with themselves. It was still early in the moon's cycle and we were all sitting on a bench on the Djema'a el-Fna drinking this *harira*-soup out of bowls. It must have been about eight and the dusk was falling rapidly. There were crowds all round us with their bowls and a huge cauldron in front from which the soup-kitchen man was ladling out the helpings. No one seemed to find it peculiar that a Christian should be amongst them.

Idrees went on: 'When the gun fires, first the *harira*, and then, after a moment, a cigarette. *Je t'offre une cigarette. Tiens!* But if I draw too much smoke into my empty body, my head will spin and I will fall to the ground, fainting. Unable to rise!'

'And soon, dinner!' Moulay Yacoub put his bowl down on the ground beside him. 'Very soon. But for some short moments we must rest our bellies after the *harira*. During the fast the belly must be treated like a child.'

We sat there for a little and then walked together on the *place*. On these *Ramadan* evenings it is so crowded that it is almost impossible to move. The cooler evening air and the relief when the fast is broken brings everyone into the open. At about nine o'clock, Moulay Yacoub and Idrees bade me good night.

'We go to our homes for the dinner,' Idrees said.

'I'm going to have mine too. Will you be coming out again afterwards?'

'Oh, no. We have our wives to attend to.'

'Wives are particularly gluttonous during the *Ramadan*,' Moulay Yacoub observed. 'And we must finish with them before the trumpet blows again.'

The trumpets are long, straight and strident and, since it is high summer, they blow again at about three o'clock. Life is rather a rush then. There is the *hammām* to be done with for those who are ritually unclean, and then an immense meal, to stoke up against the hours of starvation that follow the dawn gun. Many of the older people stay awake for fear that they may fall asleep so profoundly that the trumpet will not rouse them and they will consequently miss the second meal. The younger ones stay up as a matter of course, so the Djema'a el-Fna is crowded all night long.

If the Marrakeshis had learnt to sublimate their emotions or thought it necessary to try, these *Ramadan* nights might be less exhausting for them. As it is, neither sublimation nor neuroses trouble their lives. A spade is a spade, neither beautiful nor disgusting; it is just one of the things that crops up all the time and has to be dealt with on an *ad hoc* basis. But for the sixteen hours of daylight throughout this month of *Ramadan*, spades are mystically forbidden, so when the evening gun fires there is a lot of leeway to be made up and the air is suddenly alive with emotion. I must say that everyone is very well-mannered and nobody gets raped, and ladies who go in fear of it have only to decline politely to have the mortification of seeing the monster in question move on, with complete indifference, to someone less fussy. In this sense, gentlemen are not very gallant hereabouts. They are however wise, and keep their wives and daughters indoors.

The repair work and renovation of Maurice D—'s pavilion have made astonishing progress during the past months and although during *Ramadan* it is unlikely that much will get done, he hopes to have everything finished within a week or two of the feast, which is due with the new moon. He has continually asked for my advice on points of principle or detail, without, of course, the least intention of doing other than he has planned already. I have consequently been able to suggest all sorts of dotty extravagances, and this has pleased both of us and changed nothing. The pavilion will be beautiful, I think. Maurice's taste is very sure and very disciplined. For the interior he speaks a lot about *espace neutre*, in which it is possible to place one or two *objets rares* so that they may be given their full significance. There will be no hint of the decorator's art, at least he hopes not.

At the end of his orchard he has his workshop and stockroom – full of material for the pavilion as soon as it is ready to receive it: antique Moorish chests, some good examples of Berber pottery that is becoming increasingly difficult to find, Hispano-Mauresque pieces, wooden cupboards painted with formal arabesques of flowers and calligraphy which gleam through the patina the years have given them. He is also busy with what he calls a *panoplie* of Moorish musical instruments, of forms beautiful in themselves and a great deal more difficult to put together than you would imagine. It is causing such a fuss that I sometimes wonder if it will ever get as far as the wide white wall in the upper room for which it is intended.

In a corner of the orchard, shaded by orange trees, stand a great many potted plants, lianas of some kind, jasmine, papyrus, what I call 'elephant ears', for the pavilion. I was amused to see sweet potatoes too. They sit in water, in those inverted-conical oil-lamps that are used in mosques, with long trailing shoots covered with leaf.

I wondered if Marrakesh would really prove capable of supporting such a business, and expressed my doubts as friends do on such occasions.

'*On verra*. I will do it to the best of my ability,' Maurice said. 'And if it brings me money, *tant mieux. Mais dans tous les cas* I believe it will keep me alive, and this is the life that pleases me. I have engaged a major-domo,' he went on. 'He is from Fez, and is *ancien militaire*. I am giving him Moorish dress not too Bakst, and he is to occupy himself with the comfort of the clients. For those that wish to come and sit in the afternoons, he will also serve *thé et cornes de gazelle*.'

'They will take the tea and buy nothing.'

'On the contrary, they will pay for the tea, and downstairs, in a little *boutique*, I shall arrange the best of the horrors that people who do not like *objets authentiques* can never resist. You will see, *mon cher*.'

I think he knows what he is about.

We were walking up and down the Djema'a el-Fna, and it was long past midnight. The clowns and storytellers were doing good business, surrounded by *Ramadan* night-farers, but between these swirling groups the surface of the *place* lay black and flare-lit. It was quite cool – I even wore a light pullover – and above us the sky was very remote. Sometimes the trumpets would blow a few isolated blasts somewhere in the city – not the great cacophony of brass that would split the night air in an hour or two to warn people of the approaching dawn.

'Now is the time for the Aguedal,' Maurice said. 'When it is empty and dark with only stars for the water to reflect. Have you seen it by night?'

'No.'

'*Pourtant les anglais ont un sens profond de la nature.* Perhaps they don't know what it is, but they feel it deeply. Do not say that they have forgotten! Do trees and emptiness and water no longer please the English?'

* * *

The month of fasting is now over – it was made hideous in its final week by a return of the *Sherghi*. To mark its end, Idrees invited some of his friends to his house for the *'Aid el-seghir* feast, and I went too. It was very unlike 'Aysha's *dyafa*, but enjoyable all the same for its quiet formality. I knew several but by no means all of the guests, and there was no *hashshish* that I was aware of.

In some ways I am sorry that life has returned to daylight. There had been something so magical about the *Ramadan* moon as it grew big and then slowly wasted away to a pale splinter that came up just before the dawn. I shall miss the trumpets, and sleep more soundly. There is still talk of a picnic in the Aguedal one of these days, but of course dates are not mentioned. It is referred to as due to take place 'after a little, a little, *Insha'Allah*'. Haroon is to come to me on the morning that is finally chosen in order to claim my subscription. He will then hasten to the market to buy meat and chickens and everything, and the belief is that the plans will thereafter work like clockwork.

The worst of the heat is over, too. They say that it is now too late in the summer for a third *coup de sherghi*, and I begin to forget that we ever suffered at all, even at the worst moments.

* * *

To my surprise, the picnic in the Aguedal took place today. Everything did work like clockwork except that Sidi 'Ali, the *calèche*-driver, had not been warned of it, so the party had to wait at the *calèche*-stand for half an hour till he should return from wherever his business had taken him. Several other drivers, being well aware of what was afoot, offered to deputize for him, but Haroon, a bustling pygmy, was in control of arrangements and stood firm: Sidi'Ali or no one.

Haroon sat on the box beside the driver, wearing a very large straw hat against the sun – of a type called, I think, *taraza* which has coloured wool bobbles on it. He had put the rest of us in the back: Moulay Yacoub, Idrees, someone else that had been thought of at the last minute, and me. The new addition was addressed as Blanchette. 'You understand the *plaisanterie*, Monsieur Peter?' Moulay Yacoub asked. 'Monsieur Blanchette is called this, meaning white, because he is black, you understand?'

Blanchette laughed: 'I hope the *makla* is good.' *Makla* is food. 'How much did you pay, Idrees? Haroon has made me pay fifty francs, but he asked seventy-five at first.'

We all smiled at each other because of Haroon's astuteness, and he must have heard what was being said because he turned round on his perch and slapped at us with a casserole-lid he was nursing.

We chatted together and Blanchette (who, Idrees says, is a great ladies' man and reputedly lusty, being so black) whistled and made '*ssss*' signals to any woman we passed. Some looked up and some didn't, but I believe that, in no matter what city, even those ladies who don't answer to whistles would still like to know who's whistling.

I knew the route well: out through the gate by the Qasbah, down along the road that follows the ramparts, into an alley long and thin as a railtrack, the *Mechouar* and then the Aguedal. I noticed that the storks were coming back to their winter quarters. Throughout the summer their nests have remained on the tops of towers and bastions. Their beaks go *tak-tak-tak-tak-tak-tak*, and Moorish children sing a song about it. They are birds of good omen, and much liked. It is very nice if they choose to build their nest on your house.

We were in the Aguedal by now, clopping sedately down the long straight roadway between the olives – such ancient olives, twisted and age-blackened like trees in a fairy story. With what precision they were planted so long ago! As we clopped by, I could see the ranks of them flicking like fan-sticks into a new pattern of alleyways with every few yards of our progress. Amongst them, tethered to trees as if at deliberately-chosen intervals, were bulls. Little white paddy-birds perched on their backs, and sometimes a bull less somnolent than the others would heave himself up, hindlegs first, then the forelegs, and stand there swinging his dewlap as if it were a velvet skirt.

'I have heard that *les espagnols* fight with such bulls,' Haroon called down to us.

'Smaller bulls than those, and more fierce,' I said.

'I will fight goats!' he cried delightedly, waving his casserole-lid. It was like a school picnic. 'And cook and eat them!'

Moulay Yacoub was looking anxiously under the carriage seat, '*Where* is the *nafekh*? Where is it?'

'*Mā tekhāf shay!*' shouted Haroon. '*I* am the man who remembers! Here!' – and leaning down, he suddenly produced an earthenware brazier from under his feet. 'I am responsible for all, *and* for the remembering! You only for the money, *yā* Moulay!'

Some time later, we had settled ourselves down under a fig tree where a watercourse and a formal tiled platform, like that of a patio without the surrounding wall, had been allowed to fall into disrepair. The platform was set in chevrons of turquoise faience. At a distance of twenty yards, a more modern channel had been built to irrigate the fruit trees. 'Ali had tethered his horse some way away. The carriage itself had been left a long way off, though at the nearest point possible to this forgotten pleasaunce.

Haroon was already busy with his preparations. We sat about waiting for the meal. Naturally it took a long time, and Moulay Yacoub had started to talk, which takes a long time too. He is charming but sometimes he talks for too long, not insisting that you listen, except to what he too calls 'the fine parts', as had Si Fulan on the night of 'Aysha's *dyafa*.

In Europe, a picnic is a deliberate attempt to simulate the simple life, and, as a rule, there is no need to simulate the discomfort. It is clear from their miniatures that the Persians did not see things this way, and neither do the Moors, though on this occasion we had no dark-eyed maidens with us. But we did have carpets and cushions, a very complete kitchen, a huge brass tripod-brazier for the tea kettle, an *'amara* and a *siniya* of brass to carry the mint tea and its paraphernalia, fly whisks and a musical box. Moulay Yacoub is middle-aged and really plumper than he should be, but he lay relaxed against the tree in a very Persian manner, a fit subject for a Persian miniaturist. He had given himself up to this *fête champêtre* – reciting verses, recounting tales of the days when horses had wings and some men the heads of horned devils. In due course we ate, congratulated Haroon (as was his due), and then the party disposed itself comfortably for sleep.

I did not sleep. There is a water channel leading off from one of the raised artificial lakes in the Aguedal, and I wandered away to it. At the point where it takes off, a platform of stones has been built up in the shadow of a tree. The channel continues along its aqueduct and some hundred yards farther falls into the trap set for it by a water mill. Under the tree it is cool and shady. The channel itself is only just wide enough for me to lie down, and deep enough to let the water flow over my shoulders. I think I must look rather silly, lying in the water channel with no clothes on and a book held clear of the stream, but this is what I have done often during the summer, and I enjoy it. I lie here in the aqueduct above the level of the surrounding orchard and read, or doze. There is no one to see me and, even if there were, I believe they would consider it a pleasant and sensible way to take a siesta.

When I had had enough, I returned to the party and found them packing up in a silence with violent undertones. I did not ask, and no one volunteered to tell me, what the matter was, and so in silence we all trooped back to the *calèche*. Only now did Sidi 'Ali choose to water his horse. I had the feeling that if I had not returned at that moment they would not have considered waiting for me because no one could have broken the silence to suggest it. We set off for home. Then suddenly, as starlings will sometimes take wing from a tree at an unheard word of command, they all started talking at once and Blanchette, without warning, struggled across my knees and struck the driver in the back. The driver swung round and did what he could with his whip – not much, in the circumstances, though the intention was murderous – and this raised shouts of anger from everyone. Thereupon Idrees and Moulay Yacoub pounced on Blanchette, which gave the driver the chance to lean down and poke at him with the butt of his whip, so Haroon clouted him with his casserole-lid and Moulay Yacoub let out a scream of fury, though I don't think he had been touched.

I have been here long enough to know what to do when this sort of thing happens. Someone has to intervene; it is traditional; and the only person available to do so was me. So I threw myself into the mêlée in order to perform my noble function. In a sense, I succeeded brilliantly. They all stopped fighting to look at me in astonished silence. Of course they started again, but only talk now – abuse, recriminations and the rest of it. The real battle was over. They did not tell me what it had been about, and I thought it best not to ask. They were worn out with talk by the time we reached the *calèche*-stand where we dispersed in silence. But I have seen Idrees since then, and he said: '*N'est-ce pas que le pique-nique était beau?*'

Derb esh-Shems (5)

NOW THAT the summer is passing, the first batches of tourists have started to arrive. Quite a lot of Moors I am acquainted with, and had always supposed to be either out of work or else gentlemen of leisure, have suddenly turned out in very spruce new *djellabas* or else American-style shirts and gabardine pants. They prove to be 'guides' when the season opens.

The tourists come and take a look at the Djema'a el-Fna, the Koutoubia and all obvious sights, and today I saw a file of them mount on camels and start out from the Wagon-lits/Cook's office for a tour of the ramparts, conducted by very convincing sheiks. They do not disturb our lives much, on present form; they only want to look and go away again, with sections ticked off in the margins of their guidebooks. Haroon tells me that American tourists are the best, and that he wishes all tourists were Americans.

'Because they are richer?' I asked.

'They are richer, yes. But they are *better*, too, because the others who are not American do not speak to me, and if they do speak to me and give me *felūs*, they drop it into my hand from above, in this manner . . . ' and he mimed a man embarrassed into alms-giving. 'Do they not know that alms-giving is blessed and a duty, and that kind speech and pardon are better than alms-giving followed by annoyance? What sort of *kafir* are such men that they do not even know this?'

'Bite them on the leg,' I counselled him.

'I would like, sometimes.'

'There will be many Americans later, perhaps,' I said to comfort him. I think that what he says is true: Americans – and, from a sense of national pride I must add also, British sailors – are less embarrassed by freaks of nature than other people.

Haroon's eyes shone with anticipation. 'Yes. *Insha' Allah*, there will be many Americans.' Then they clouded over again. 'Do you think that if I wore new clothes they would wish me for a guide? This *djellaba* is become a little old, *yak*?' He was busy refitting a triangular rent into position, but it gaped open again as soon as he let it go. The poor little *djellaba* was disgracefully shabby and old.

'Don't waste new clothes on tourists, Haroon. Save the new clothes for the *'Aid el-Kebīr.*' The mutton-feast will be fairly soon now. New clothes will be very important then.

'But I have none for the *'Aid el-Kebīr*,' he murmured sadly.

* * *

It was inevitable that one of these days one of these tourists would be known to me, but it has happened sooner than I had expected. An Englishman I shall call Brandon has arrived, with his wife. We met on the *place.*

'Well for the love of Mike, if it isn't Peter Mayne!' he cried, and came quickly forward as if he were truly glad to see me. This sort of thing is infectious and I felt pleased, though I had known him only slightly and that a long way off in time and interest. I hadn't met his wife. She looked attractive and a good deal younger than he was.

'Brandon! How nice to see you!'

He introduced me to his wife. 'Are you here for long? Where are you staying?' I asked her.

'At the Mamounia,' she said. 'How nice to meet old friends of Ralph's.' (Ralph! That was the name, of course.) 'Are you at the Mamounia too?'

I can't remember ever thinking of myself as one of Brandon's friends. We had met over a short period before the war and had been quite happy to see each other in the company of mutual acquaintances – at a bar for instance – but that was about all.

'No. Not the Mamounia.'

'You must come and have dinner with us,' she said. She was really very amiable, and so was he. Perhaps they felt out of things on this mad African *place* and were glad to find someone connected with their real lives, however remotely. 'It's so amusing, isn't it? So *strange*!' She was indicating a group of Sudani singers. Their leader winked at me and came forward, a grubby little cap in his hand. 'What should I give him?' she asked me.

'Oh!' I was looking her over and noted a fine jewelled clip on her lapel. 'Whatever you like. Fifty francs would be generous.'

'Let's be really generous then. Ralph darling, give me a hundred for this man, will you?'

'A hundred? Isn't that rather a lot . . . ?' He looked at me inquiringly, 'I mean . . . '

It was a very great deal too much, of course, and I felt ashamed of myself, but the Sudani was pleased and I soon forgot about it.

'What are you doing this evening, old man?'

'Nothing. Nothing in particular.'

'Then come and dine with us. About eight. Okay? In the lounge at the Mamounia. Don't bother to change, no one does.' He glanced down at my jeans and added, 'Just any old suit, you know.'

I went to dine with them. I even put on a suit in their honour, and by the time we were drinking coffee and cognac on the terrace outside the restaurant I was feeling very well-disposed towards them. I had been doubtful hitherto, not because I liked or disliked them, but because they were my first link in months with a different sort of earlier existence, and the two things are, after all, quite separate. He had been telling me at length all that had happened to him since we had met. I cannot pretend that it interested me much, but the dinner had been good, and they were friendly, kind people.

'And now that I've put you in the picture, old man, tell me about yourself.'

'Yes do, Mr Mayne. Are you on a long trip? When did you leave England?'

'Oh, I'm just living here, you know.'

'Living? You don't mean indefinitely?'

'Yes. For ever, I hope.'

'How *exciting*! Oh, I think that it must be terribly romantic to live here!' Mrs Brandon clasped her hands together and looked up into the sky. For the moment, she really meant it.

'Well, isn't that interesting! What do you do? – if I'm not being indiscreet, that is.'

'Well, I write . . . and I . . . I just live here and . . . write.'

'Good God! I mean that's new, isn't it? I didn't know about that. Since when is all this? Let's see, you were doing a government job then, weren't you? Useful officer you were too, old Wargrave used to tell me . . . '

'Wargrave? Who's Wargrave?'

'Wargrave? Wouldn't it have been him then?'

'I can't think of anyone of that name.'

'Then it must have been someone else . . . ' Brandon's voice tailed off in uncertainty. He had been trying to say something nice and now looked embarrassed. I could imagine him saying to his wife afterwards, 'Well, that was a blob all right, wasn't it, dear?'

'Anyway it's only since then,' I said.

'Only since – what? Sorry, old chap, I've rather lost the plot.'

'Only since that time that I've been writing.'

'Should we know your work, Mr Mayne? Do you write books and things, I mean?'

'I don't see how you could know about me.'

'Anyway, it's all very interesting.' Brandon said brightly and then, with a quick, thankful change of tone, 'So you must know Marrakesh pretty well by now. We must get Mr Mayne to show us round, mustn't we, darling?'

'Indeed we must! Will you, Mr Mayne?'

I suppose I said 'Yes, of course ', but with that blank in the back of my mind which means that I shall find it impossible to do anything of the sort. I had started to dislike Brandon, quite unjustifiably.

'At all events you *look* happy enough,' Brandon commented. He was leaning forward over the table and I felt that he was trying not to say something that, nevertheless, he was going to say. 'But don't you feel out of touch, don't you miss the old life sometimes? Of course I know it's romantic, as Doris says, and all that – but just sometimes don't you long for all the things you're missing?'

Probably he expected me to say 'Yes, yes . . . ' or even 'No, no!', but he had caught me unawares. What sort of things did he mean? My failure to come in on cue upset him, I think, and he started burbling on: 'I mean when *so* much is happening in the modern world and . . . and everywhere – to come and bury yourself out here, back in the Middle Ages – though the French have done wonders, I'll give you that. Remarkable. And Lyautey. Great man . . . and . . . Yes, and another thing! When you do come back you'll feel a stranger in your own country!' I think that's what he was saying, or something like it. My mind had stuck at an earlier point.

'I don't believe I miss anything, Brandon,' I said.

He patted me on the shoulder. 'What's wrong with "Ralph", old man? Call me Ralph! Well, surely . . . Live on here for ever . . . ? It's not quite the same thing here as in Europe, after all. You'll go rusty if you don't take care, and that would never do! Nothing to sharpen your wits on, eh?'

'Quite honestly I don't think I miss anything. Nothing I mind about, in any case.'

I managed to laugh it off somehow and we had another cognac. I didn't want to discuss my life with him, and I'm sure he could not have wanted to either so, without much difficulty, I steered the conversation back to themselves and their holiday trip. He jumped at the bait and the recital carried us through this cognac and another one to follow it. We were all a good deal mellower by now, but I wanted to go. I looked surreptitiously at my watch and saw that it was after eleven. So I started to get to my feet with an apologetic expression: 'It's time for me to go, I'm afraid.'

'Oh no! Stay and have a nightcap. The night's young yet.'

'No, really. I think I must . . . '

'Now *why*? Come on – sit down again, d'you hear? A-ha-ha! You can't leave us yet! Don't pretend you're going to settle down to write at this hour!' He smiled roguishly. 'I begin to believe there's something else, old man. Some little French girl, you know, eh?' He actually dug me in the ribs. 'Waiter!'

And then, when another cognac came, he put me through a jocular interrogation. The cognac, far from helping, made me stubborn. Why should I tell him my private affairs, even as a joke? Why? I refused to do so. He wouldn't understand anyhow. But he badgered me, trying to bring his wife into the game too and finally I lost my head and cried, 'Listen! Do you really want to know why I have come here to live? Do you want to know? Yes? Because I suddenly realized that I was an illiterate intellectual! That's why!'

They looked at each other in astonishment.

'*And* over-civilized,' I added sharply.

'*Over-civilized* . . . ? What do you mean, old man?'

Mrs Brandon tapped her husband nervously on the wrist. 'I think Mr Mayne means that the life of the intellect is not enough, dear.'

Silly anxious woman! Kind, good woman too, only wanting to help – but I was past helping.

'Yes!' I went on, much too loudly. 'Over-civilized! And you are too! We've been caught up in our brilliant little world of progress and prophylaxis and can't see that the only way to make that tolerable would be to *have* an intellect and a life of it. But we haven't *got* intellects, you and I! So what does that make us? Just sillies with insurance policies against life or death, and instincts bound up in insulating tape!'

They sat back and looked at each other, wagging their heads slowly, with their eyes saying 'mad . . . mad . . . mad . . . !' Then Mrs Brandon had a brain-wave. She had of course quite lost whatever sympathy she may have felt for me earlier. 'So you've gone back to nature, Mr Mayne.'

That stopped the nonsense all right. She made me sound like a self-conscious nudist. And at that moment Maurice came on to the terrace. I cannot imagine what he could have been doing there, but there he was, a lifebelt.

'Maurice!' I cried.

He looked round and waved.

'An old friend,' I said happily, turning to Mrs Brandon. 'I didn't even know he was in Morocco.'

'Like us, eh?' Brandon tried to smile.

'Well, not . . . Yes, just like you.' I felt I couldn't bear another moment with the Brandons. 'I wonder if you'd think me very rude if . . . '

'No, er . . . not in the least. Mr Mayne . . . If you feel you ought to. Not in the least.' She swallowed and added in a voice she could not prevent sounding cold, 'How small the world is.'

'Yes, isn't it? Well? If you really won't think me . . . I think I'll just . . . It was so kind of you, Mrs Brandon. I have so much enjoyed the evening. Thank you, Brandon – Ralph, I mean. I'll telephone, shall I? And we'll . . . '

I backed away from them, angry with myself yet relieved, because it was all over now and I need never see them again.

I went up to Maurice, took him by the arm and steered him away.

'Why are you so pink?' Maurice asked. 'And what are you doing here in a suit?'

* * *

Yesterday evening at sundown I suddenly saw 'Aysha walking past the Café de France with 'Abdeslem. I have been very preoccupied recently, forcing my reluctant faculties to apply themselves to the novel. Consequently I am out of touch with events in Derb esh-Shems and had heard nothing of 'Abdeslem's unbewitchment, yet he certainly looked more or less unbewitched now, and 'Aysha's eyes were shining over the top of her veil.

'*Tout va bein*,' she called out to me, taking 'Abdeslem's arm in a very proprietary manner as they went by. 'Abdeslem acknowledged my greeting and even smiled a little. Then 'Aysha must have instructed him to do something or other, for he nodded weakly and hesitated, and she gestured at him and he walked on, muttering to himself, while 'Aysha turned and came towards me in triumph.

'So you unbewitched him, 'Aysha,' I said. 'How did you do it?'

'You wish to know?' she asked. '*Tout ce qu'il y a de simple.* I took myself to the *pharmacie.*'

'The ostrich, I suppose . . . ?'

'The ostrich – pah! He is for other things. No. *La pharmacie.* The biggest *pharmacie*, that in the *Ville Nouvelle.* The best!'

'But 'Aysha! Do European people know enough about such matters?'

She waved me aside. 'I begged them to give me some medicament for causing a gentleman to vomit. The most expensive. *This* is what they gave me.' She produced a little bottle, two-thirds empty now. I pulled the cork and smelt it. I think it must have been ipecacuanha.

'How did you cause him to take it?'

'How? I first made certain promises to the night-watchman. In due course, the promises fulfilled, he called 'Abdeslem. I then told 'Abdeslem that this medicament had been supplied by a Berber lady for his cure. Such was his condition, *le pauvre jeune homme* (for it is many, many weeks now, is it not?) that he was ready to take anything. And *pfff!* He vomited the evil away!'

'And he is really all right again now?' It was rather an anticlimax. I had been hoping for something richer – and to be present at the séance myself.

'Nearly all right. And profoundly grateful. For my part I have informed him that for so long as he continues *honnête et bien* the evil is unlikely to lodge itself again within him. Soon he is to open his charcoal *boutique* once more. Monsieur Peter, I think it will now be proper for you to buy your charcoal from 'Abdeslem as in the past.'

* * *

Maurice tells me that a certain Madame T., whom I met some time ago at Mlle de V.'s '*réunion*', is obliged to return to France for family reasons, leaving her Marrakesh house empty. She does not like the idea of abandoning it in this way and would be glad of a *gardien* during the months of her absence. He has suggested my name to her.

'*Cela vous intéresserait*, Peter?' He knows that Derb esh-Shems is not perfect and has rather excited me by saying that Madame T.'s house has running water. 'And since it is free of rent, you can perhaps afford a domestic.' Madame T. is evidently not leaving her own domestic, as the woman is sick, but there is a Moorish girl known to Madame T. who could look after me if I wish.

All this was several days ago now, and since then I have been to see Madame T. (who is charming) and her house (which is charming too). The house is certainly small, but it has running water, and a flush closet – Turkish style – and a shower over the closet, and even a bathtub concealed behind a screen, though that is in the bedroom. I gave the bed a thump when Madame T. wasn't looking, and was happy to find that it has a spring base and a spring overlay mattress. One way and another, the thought of moving in pleases me a great deal. The proposal has also involved talking to my landlord at Derb esh-Shems and, by some magical coincidence, he seems quite pleased that I should vacate the house, because he wants to use it for relatives. So my going suits everybody concerned. I shall certainly take on the girl Madame T. has proposed. Her pay will be nearly covered by saving on the rent, and then she can do the marketing and the cooking and the household wash and I shall have more leisure than ever.

It will be sad saying goodbye to Derb esh-Shems because I have become fond of my neighbours, but it is a good exchange and, after all, the neighbours can visit me. Anyhow they say they will, and it all leaves a very nice taste in the mouth. I am also overjoyed at being freed from a suitcase as a writing-desk.

*　*　*

I am to move tomorrow. A man who lives at the end of Derb esh-Shems hopes, God willing, to be with his handcart at my door at eight o'clock to carry my baggage. We shall walk together, pushing the handcart, to the new house which is just off the Riad ez-Zitoun within shouting distance of the Djema'a el-Fna. Fifty francs, he says, since we are neighbours, and since my new house is so near the place where, in any event, he must push his handcart to wait for custom. 'Aysha is to come in this evening to help clean up my present house and she has also made a sort of cake. She laughingly says that she has put nothing powerful in it because I should already be a kilometre away when it could be expected to start working.

'If it were a posset and not a cake,' she explains, 'then distance would not matter. The posset *stops* things. The pink cakes *start* things and though the person eating them is supposed to desire some named other person after he has eaten them, it is necessary for that other person to be close at hand to receive the desire. Otherwise the cakes may work wrongly. So do not fear anything, Monsieur Peter.'

For my part I have given 'Aysha one of my two tin buckets (no more jaunts to the water-point, thank Heaven!) and to 'Abdeslem I have given a shirt he has long coveted. Since the unbewitchment, 'Abdeslem is very amenable and ready to accept anything. This particular shirt has been in my possession for many years and I now consider it too young for me. The night-watchman has his eyes on an old sweater – or else a plastic mug, he says. With the coming of the cooler weather, he often makes tea for himself during the silent night hours and at present he has only a '*Petits Pois, NORA*' tin for drinking out of.

I am moving to a much smarter quarter and this has impressed Derb esh-Shems. The handcart man has promised the others to take note of where my house is so that he can tell them, and in this way they expect to be able to find it and visit me as soon as I have had time to settle in.

4

Riad ez-Zitoun

THE OLIVE GARDEN – that is what the name means – is proving a great success. To be strictly truthful, Madame T.'s house is not in the Olive Garden itself but in an alley leading from it, which twists like a Chelsea bun till it comes to my front door. Nor is the Olive Garden more than a road of that name – no trees, no fruit, just a busy little road. Never mind, I very much like Madame T.'s house and the patio, the comfortable bed, the kitchen, the well-stocked linen-cupboard, and the sitting-room where I can have my meals and write without the misery of clearing away one mess to make room for another. The little Moorish girl who looks after me, Brīka, is adequate but a 'simple' child. I have had to be presented to her father for a sort of security check and he seems to have decided that I will do. His decision is based on assurances and guarantees from Idrees and others. 'Abdeslem has already paid me a visit, and I suspect that it was primarily in order to look poor Brīka over. She did not please him – which is a mercy. He told me so. He also says that until he feels quite strong again he will not be reopening his charcoal-shop. He will rest for a bit and is taken with the idea of spending some part of each day on my comfortable bed, while I write next door. I have turned down this idea.

'It is not reposeful in 'Aysha's house,' he says.

I can imagine that this is the case, but I am learning to please myself in such matters without either reference to other people's wishes or the least twinge of guilt. In days gone by, I have pleased myself and felt guilty as well, so it will be seen that I am making progress.

'Moreover, I shall talk in Arabic with you,' 'Abdeslem continued, ignoring my decision. 'In this way you will very soon speak the tongue well.'

Even this temptation I can resist. My Arabic is improving as it is, and my first need is to get the novel finished in the hope that it may earn me a little money. 'When my book is finished perhaps I shall start working on Arabic again, 'Abdeslem.'

'Book . . . ? Monsieur Peter, will you please teach me to work that *makīna*, the blessing of God be on you?' My typewriter fascinates him. This is not the first time he has asked me to teach him to work it, nor the first time he has declined to believe that he must first learn to read and write. The typewriter possesses for him the same magical properties as an amulet.

I have barred my door to 'Abdeslem henceforth except on invitation. I do not really want him to repose himself about the place, and I don't trust him with poor Brīka. She is plain and 'simple', but he might start feeling sorry for her, and it is I who am responsible to her father.

* * *

Brīka flies about the house in a disconcerting manner, her arms full of washing, or with buckets and brooms and so on. She may not be very pretty, but she seems honest, clean and willing. She wears baggy drawers in pink-and-white stripes which fasten below the knee, but they are only really visible in moments of great exertion, when her movements makes her overskirts billow upwards. Her topmost skirt is drawn up in front and stuffed into her belt so that the second skirt shows in a panel in front. Without being at all like a Dresden shepherdess, the effect of panniers is there, with naked calves under them, and a bosom above held in by a system of crossed cords over her blouse. She wears the inevitable *sibnīya* – the headscarf El-Meknasi was forever talking about.

When Brīka goes out – as she does each day after breakfast to get in supplies of ice, bread and kerosene for the cooking-stove – she puts on her *hāik*. This is a rectangle of heavy, white cotton cloth. By catching it at some point near the middle and fastening it with a cord, she has the beginnings of an overcoat. The cord is passed over her shoulder, the white cotton folds are draped over her head and around the breast and hips, and one of the hems is held across her nose in such a manner that nothing of poor little Brīka remains visible but one bright eye and her ankles. Her eyes are her best feature, they shine and smoulder with vitality. Her ankles and feet are her worst. She is willing, but she is stupid to a point that neither threats nor tears can reach. I find that I cannot leave her to buy our food; I have to go to the market myself to choose. Her cooking is almost as bad as mine.

* * *

Maurice and Mlle de V. came in yesterday evening for an aperitif. I hesitate to call it a 'house-warming'. Maurice was rather silent because he is in the midst of opening his pavilion for business. He doesn't take alcohol, so he had coffee, while Mlle de V. and I sipped cinzano and 'Old Lady's gin'. In the ordinary way, she accepts nothing from anybody, so profound is her need for independence, but an aperitif in a private house – yes, perhaps. Cigarettes are different, even matches.

'*Merci, merci!*' she cries, scrabbling in her bag for her lighter, as if my matches might be poisoned. '*J'ai mon briquet. Ah! Le voilà.*'

'And what is your news, mademoiselle?'

She looked at her hands and said, '*Eh bien*, there *is* news, *mais . . . Assez curieux, du reste*. You wish me to tell you?'

'But of course! Please tell me at once.'

'Alors. *Vous vous souvenez de la poule bressane et la dinde?*'

'I remember them very well indeed.'

'Imagine to yourself then that these two now sit upon a *bouton de porte! Elles couvent toutes les deux le même bouton de porte!*'

Even Maurice came out of his reverie for a moment at this. '*Un bouton de porte?*'

'A doorknob? How very peculiar,' I said. 'But why . . . ? Who gave it to them? What happened to their eggs? Surely they must notice some difference.' It is sometimes a little difficult to be sure that Mlle de V. is not playing an elaborate joke, but she has the habit of proving the truth of her statements.

'Exactly,' said Mlle de V. '*Un bouton de porte en porcelaine.* Flower-painted. After what had befallen they had need of something of the kind, I think.'

'What *had* happened, mademoiselle? You forget that I am very out of date with the news.'

She looked out into the patio. Madame T. has planted three banana trees which grow so rapidly that one can almost see the leaves opening from their sheaths. Later they will hide the washing-line on the roof; at present they seem to point derisively towards it. Mlle de V. lowered her gaze again.

'You will remember that they would sit, side by side, on their nest, waiting for the eggs to hatch? Never, never would they leave their nest both at the same time, for fear of marauders. If the *poule bressane* had need to walk a little under the trees, the *dinde* would remain guarding. It was beautiful to see. But one day they both left the nest together . . . '

It happened, Mlle de V. said, that on that afternoon she was walking under the trees at the end of the *riad*, and, seeing the nest empty, tiptoed forward to examine the eggs, *la bressane's* four, *la dinde's* two. The birds were scrabbling about in the undergrowth nearby and she could hear them clucking as she approached. They were understandably nervous of any creature that walked in the vicinity and so came hastening after her. Imagine Mlle de V.'s dismay to find all but one of the six eggs smashed to pieces! '*Brutalisés d'une façon atroce!*' she cried. '*Sauf un seul!*' The poor birds were horrified too. They flapped and squawked and behaved like the distracted mothers they were.

'I do not think either could face the possibility that all was lost to her,' Mlle de V. went on, 'and the consequences therefore explain themselves. Both mothers claimed the sole survivor as her own.'

'But surely . . . ?'

'Monsieur, you are making ready to say that the egg of a *bressane* can be distinguished from that of a *dinde*. Am I right? Certainly. And you are right, too. Yet this one egg was perhaps the largest of the four little ones, and at the same time it could have been the smaller of the two big ones. There was room for doubt in a heart that otherwise must break.'

'Could *you* not distinguish then, mademoiselle?'

'Naturally *I* could distinguish, my eyes being unblurred by tragedy. It was a *bressane* egg that remained. But *la dinde* did not wish to believe this. That is what I am obliged to suppose.' She shook her head and smiled. '*Quelle histoire étrange, n'est-ce pas?* And from that moment until the birth, they both sat upon this one egg *à tour de role*. In turns.'

'And then?'

'The babe emerged.'

'*A bressane?*'

'*Naturellement une bressane*. In part *bressane, tout au moins*. What did you expect, monsieur? *Un serpent?*'

'I had not thought of a serpent, mademoiselle, but knowing what I know, nothing would surprise me in the matter of your fowls.'

'It was not a serpent, but a chicken. And perhaps the only beautiful circumstance of the whole *récit* is this, that *la dinde* at once relinquished her claim while continuing to accord her devotion. As you are doubtless aware, monsieur, chickens are able to walk and peck at the grains from the moment of leaving the shell. You are also aware that my *riad* harbours many cats, and amongst them some that may not be trusted with fledglings. You understand? *Eh bien*, with what does *la dinde* charge herself? The provision of *garde du corps* for this beloved chick! As the true mother would strut among the pebbles, the chick at her side, so *la dinde* would follow at a discreet distance, and watchful. Once I was astonished to see *la dinde* floating in the air above her two *protégées, comme un immense lit de plume protecteur* – though she was unable to float for long. Nor, alas, was it availing. Within two days the chick was no more . . .'

'Not dead? You mean these cats got it in the end?'

'Cats? Ah no . . . At least I think not. I *fear* not.'

'Then what do you fear, mademoiselle?' I asked.

She didn't answer my question. Instead she went on with her story which apparently was not yet finished. 'So now they sit in hope or desperation upon a *bouton de porte en porcelaine*. Do you not find that peculiar?'

'Perhaps it was the kindest thing you could have done.'

'I?'

'Yes. I think you did right. The poor fowls seem to be fated one way or another, don't they?'

'I? You suggest it was I who gave them the button? *Nullement!* They discovered it. And rolled it back to the nest. They are now profoundly attached to it and have time for nothing else.'

'And the cockerel? What about him? What does he think of the button?'

'The *coq* dislikes the button and has returned to the little *pavillon en bois* where he now lives tranquilly with *la poule paralysée*.'

I sat back and said: 'Ah–h! Now I understand.'

'Do you?' Mlle de V. asked, looking at me closely. 'Of course I am sorry for *l'affligée* but from the beginning I could quite comprehend that the *coq* should prefer *la bressane*. But, do you know, the Berber woman who cleans for me says that *l'affligée* is a witch? *Une sorcière*.'

I said: 'You do not need to be a Berber woman who cleans for you in order to know that.'

Mlle de V. nodded wisely. '*Parfaitement, monsieur. Je suis de votre avis.* I have felt it for months, but now, apart from her affliction, I do not like to . . . to cause anything to happen to *la poule paralysée* for the sake of the neighbourhood. Already there is a transparent *lalla* in our *quartier* who awaits late-farers, her eyes shining under the moon. *La paralysée après tout* gives me eggs – she is not ill-disposed towards human beings, I think . . . at present . . .'

Maurice, who had paid little attention to this sombre story, now broke in, '*Le bouton de porte mademoiselle. Dîtes-moi, vous n'avez donc pas la paire . . . ? De quelle coulour est-ce?* I was thinking, if you had two . . .'

I told him to shut up and Mlle de V. pretended not to have heard.

* * *

It would be silly to pretend that Brīka is a very neat mender. She darns my socks with cotton thread, drawing the rents together and overstitching them into firm, straight ridges. I have begged her to choose at least the right colour, from a plait of darning-wools (my socks being wool) that I have bought her expressly for this purpose, but she countered with an explanation she didn't even wish me to understand, and has continued with her contrasting-overstitch technique. Similarly, with some sheets of mine that have grown tender with use, I have explained – very largely in mime – that she should give them to some sewing-woman who should be asked to split them down the middle and machine them together again, sides to centre. It would be an excellent opportunity to have this done while I am in Madame T.'s house and using her sheets. Brīka nodded as one might nod to an acquaintance, and when my back was turned attacked the split sections with darning-wool, sky-blue. I have therefore been obliged to search for a sewing-woman myself, and have now delivered the sheets, including the one repaired by Brīka, to a young Jewish maiden whom I have discovered with two others in a booth not very far from where I live.

The booth is wide open to the street and about two feet above ground level. It is a recess in the wall, as it were, and some four square yards in area, covered with matting. On the matting the three Jewish maidens sit, cross-legged and comfy, operating their sewing-machines. Two of the maidens are pretty – joyful, with thick tresses of shiny hair. They have eyes that are as big and slumbrous as black olives. People stand about outside the booth watching them, but they take no notice. The third maiden is less pretty – in fact no one could call her pretty at all unless youth is in itself beautiful, which I doubt. She is a very heavy little girl, seventeen perhaps, and let's face it; she is plain.

Of the three, I deliberately chose the third, whose name is Miriam – a good, antique, Biblical name. I feel in some dim way that the plainer the girl, the better the seamstress.

Miriam clicked her tongue over Brīka's mending and we agreed that the sheet already repaired should be at double charge, so as to include the time taken to unpick the sky-blue ridges. I have also given Miriam a length of cloth bought recently from a street barrow to make a shirt for me. She gave the shirt I was wearing a very professional look, fingered the collar, examined the way in which the back was set into the yoke and said she could – for so much. I am to give her my shirt to copy. She seems a good, sensible girl.

While this was going on, the other two giggled and whirled their machines. This they do by delivering a series of sharp rotatory slaps to the fly-wheel – they disdain the handle. Possibly my miming of a little handle that must be ceaselessly turned confused Brīka and made it difficult for her to understand what I meant. Brīka's native tongue is '*chelha*' (the Berber language) and her Arabic is jumbled. But I believe still that her incomprehension was deliberate.

Two of the sewing-girls have Singer sewing-machines. Miriam's is an old but still serviceable Pfaff. We shall see what she can do with it.

* * *

Brīka came to me in tears after breakfast and said: 'I cannot . . . *I* want to, but my head keeps saying "No, no!" '

'You cannot *what*, Brīka?' I could see how her poor head was saying 'No, no!', waggling unhappily from side to side, but I didn't know why.

'I cannot work,' she sobbed, and fled away into the kitchen. I didn't know what to do. I felt so sorry for her that after a moment I followed her into the kitchen, to try to comfort her and at the same time to discover exactly what was wrong.

'You mean you cannot work for me? Am I so bad to you?'

'No, no . . . '

'Then what is the matter, Brīka? Don't cry! What *is* the matter?'

But she wouldn't tell me. I am not sure that she even knew herself. I have had to let her go. There's no battling against Brīka's head, after all. I have sent a message to her father telling him what has happened. Brīka did manage to say that perhaps she will come back with the new moon, but I don't think I really want her back, if I can find someone more reliable, and I have had to explain this to her father too.

What I want, of course, is an elderly woman, someone fat and placid whose head does not distress her. I shall ask my Moorish friends to recommend somebody. Meanwhile I shall manage somehow. The only real problem during the time that I am servantless will be the household wash.

* * *

I fetched the sheets from Miriam this afternoon, and the shirt. The sheets will pass, but the shirt is awful and I don't like to speak of it. I shall put it aside and perhaps one day it will make a present for somebody. Miriam has done her best, of that I am sure, but . . . well, anyway, I prefer not to think of it and I am afraid she sensed what was going on in my mind because a look of awful mortification came over her. One of these days she is going to turn that look on a husband who finds himself unable to face some loving sweetmeat on which she has lavished all her skill. It was unbearable. I felt that in spite of all I must find means of showing her that I had not lost confidence in her as a person. So I told her about Brīka's head and the household-wash problem that has resulted. At this, she brightened up immediately and suggested, to my surprise, that her mother might be happy to visit me once a week to deal with the wash until I get a new servant. I would have to supply the soap, the *eau de javel* and the electric iron; Madame Z. (her mother), the skilled hands.

Even in Marrakesh 'at once' will occasionally seem a better time for doing dullish things than some time in the vague future, so I asked Miriam for her mother's address and went at once to visit her. She lives in a two-roomed lodging in the Mellah. The Mellah is the Jewish quarter of a Moorish city, and the word derives from the Arabic consonantal root MLH – 'salt'. The form 'Mellah' means 'the place of salting' and has to do with the salting of severed heads, in order to preserve them (for spikes on the Djema'a el Fna in the case of Marrakesh). The Jewish people were required to do the salting. Hereabouts, the Muslims were always the executioners. At all events, salted the heads had to be in earlier days.

Madame Z. lives in the Mellah in these two tiny rooms of which I could only catch a glimpse through the front door. The alley leading to it is so narrow that even bicycle traffic is prohibited. She lives there with her husband and seven of their ten children, three being already married and established in the world. All this Madame Z. told me, adding that an eleventh tot is expected soon, but not so soon that she will not first have been able to complete two weekly washes for me. She is a very nice woman and speaks a flowing French. Miriam resembles her unmistakably, and I think perhaps they both have the kind of looks which better suit maturity than the burgeoning of youth. I did not meet Monsieur Z., but Madame Z. spoke of him. He has a fatigued heart, she says, and cannot work. Nor can I see why he should work so long as he is able to give Madame Z. the priceless gift of children, who will do so instead.

'Ours is a strict home,' she said. 'All my children have been brought up as they should be. Soon my Miriam will be ripe for marriage. I will come tomorrow for the first wash.'

The agreement was sealed with a cup of thick, black coffee upon her doorstep.

* * *

Madame Z. came according to plan on Thursday and within a matter of hours had washed everything, dried much of it on our terrace and ironed some, all with tremendous efficiency. I was working in the sitting-room, she was at a tub in the patio. It is not a tub, as a matter of fact, but a gigantic pottery saucer, glazed on the inside, about five foot across. She places this on the ground and seems to find no difficulty in bending double to knead and squeeze the linen. Nor does this prevent her from talking all the time. There is now no intimate detail of the Z. family life that I do not know and remember, because she is a talker who exacts responses from her listener to make sure he is attending.

At intervals I made my responses: '*Tiens, Madame Z.! . . .*'

'*Pas possible! . . .*'

'*On n'aurait jamais cru!*'

But she is a very nice woman. Apart from her daughter Miriam, I think she is the first Moroccan Israelite that I have really met. She is admirable, and very down to earth. From what I have seen of the Mellah, there can be no private life in those teeming airless alleyways, so Madame Z. has never acquired the habit of reticence. Her mind runs ceaselessly upon chastity and the future wedded bliss of her daughters. Miriam is the eldest unmarried, and is therefore the next to go through the hoop.

'A *good* girl. She is to be trusted implicitly. You may find it strange, monsieur, that I permit her to work at her Pfaff there before all those men who regard. You do? No? Well, even if you did, then *phui*! – I *fiche* myself of it and them! Miriam is well able to protect herself. She carries a little knife and a *Main de Fatima* in gold between her breasts. On a golden chain. She is well aware that when the smiling day of her marriage comes she will have nothing to bring her husband as dowry except her Pfaff and what she has been able to earn from it (*en parenthèses*, I may tell you that her Pfaff formed part of my own dowry twenty-five years ago – I was a bride at fifteen), *and* her chastity. I have brought her up to know that a woman's virtue is beyond all price. I am determined that she shall have a husband who is able to appreciate it. You agree, monsieur?'

'Wholeheartedly, madame.'

'*Exactement.* She is a *good* girl. From the age of fourteen when first I entrusted to her the Pfaff, she has been earning, and has obliged me to accept some contribution to the expenses of our home. It is touching, and indeed acceptable. Soon, if God wills it, she shall find the man fated to be hers. There is for example a good neighbour who has a *commerce* mending the pots and the pans; he has a son, fine, healthy, honourable . . . '

She also told me many little anecdotes about her children, how they would do this and that innocuous thing, and respect their father and their mother. There is something rather splendid about Madame Z. She left me after lunch, but returned later to complete the ironing of the garments which had not dried out during her first session.

But in spite of Madame Z.'s excellence, I hope I shall soon find a new servant. Even the doubtful efficiency of a Brīka has enriched my life by leaving me free to do as I please and, having tasted blood, I can't do without it. Of course I hope too that the new woman will be better than Brīka, and Idrees, Moulay Yacoub, Maurice, Mlle de V., even Haroon and others, have all been prevailed upon to keep their eyes open for someone suitable. I have not spoken to 'Aysha about it, nor even seen her recently.

* * *

I have taken to feeding in restaurants again in order to save myself the fuss of marketing and cooking. On principle, I settle down to writing after breakfast, but I notice I have a tendency to go out to lunch a good hour before it is time to do so; and then, having fed, I have found myself walking in a big garden near the Koutoubia. It is true that sometimes I scribble a few notes under a tree, but much more true that the sun and the sky are irresistible. How beautiful the autumn sun is! The air is clean and limpid and I forget that I ought to be scribbling and, when I remember again; I say to myself that as soon as I have a servant to market and cook for me, I shall revert to meals in the house and regular working hours.

* * *

A disaster seemed to have happened yesterday, and I don't think I would record it if I did not already know the sequel, which is a triumph. It concerns not me but the Z. family.

Yesterday was Madame Z.'s second washday at my house. She arrived very late and in a state of madness. Her hair was flying about and her face was streaked with tears, both dried and fresh. She wasn't alone, either. Several anxious sympathizers had followed her to my door, but as soon as she was inside she slammed it in their faces and made as if to faint. I managed to support her to the divan and lowered her on to it.

She took a deep breath, seemed not even to hear what I was trying to say to her, and started, 'Monsieur! Ah, monsieur! *O malédiction, malédiction!* How am I now punished for my brave presumptuous speech! Ah tragedy . . . ! *Quel désastre!*' She flung her arms across her forehead, shivered, and looked up again in horror. 'I can stay but a minute. At any moment now perhaps my darling will speak! But in case she does not, I fly *à toute allure à la pharmacie de la Paix* for salts to put beneath her nose. These salts will cause her to speak and we shall know the worst! But already I *know* the worst! *Le pire, monsieur, c'est le pire!*'

At this point she broke down again, and I had to comfort her, this big, blowsy, lovable woman in anguish. But she pulled herself together, sniffing and searching for a handkerchief. I gave her mine. '*Merci,*' she whispered in a tiny exhausted voice. '*Vous êtes gentil. Alors* . . . figure to yourself that my little one . . . ' And she broke down again.

'Come, madame,' I said. 'Let me call in one of those ladies who are battering at the door. She will remain with you here, and I can then fly to the *pharmacie* for the salts. Let me first give you a sip of cognac and . . . '

'No!' she cried, and then, after a second's thought, 'Perhaps, however, if you will accompany me to the *pharmacie* . . . But no, for I should never have the courage to tell you, there in the public street, yet tell I am obliged to, for how else can you help me? Monsieur, I require your help.' With a great effort the poor woman composed herself a little. 'Here, within these four walls I will tell you . . . '

I fetched her a cognac and she sipped it.

'Last night my . . . my child Miriam requests permission of her father to visit the bioscope in the company of the married daughter of a neighbour. This is not the first occasion on which permission has been granted for such a purpose – the neighbour's married daughter is above reproach, the *pellicule "Dumbo"* is harmless, Miriam is, *après tout*, sixteen. Only sixteen and . . . ' Madame Z.'s lips were quivering. I patted her hand. 'Go on, *chère madame*,' I said. She drew her breath in shakily.

'She decked herself, *la pauvre petite*, requested the pendant that belonged to my mother, and bade us *bon soir. Bon soir?* And what then?' Madame Z. approached her face to mine and hissed, 'Well may you ask! The hour for the *sortie* from the bioscope arrives, and a half-hour beyond it. Miriam has not returned. I glance anxiously at Monsieur Z. and he returns the glance similarly anxious. Then he rises, leaves the house to visit that of the neighbour's daughter. The lady is already in bed, *endormie*. "*Non, Monsieur Z.*," she murmurs from her window. "Miriam is not here. *Je ne l' ai pas vue depuis hier.*" Not seen my angel since yesterday? Then what has befallen? Is my child a . . . ?'

'Never,' I said emphatically.

Madame Z. rounded on me furiously. 'But she *is*! Wait, monsieur! Please do not interrupt. Back in our home we wait. We wait an hour, two hours. Monsieur Z. runs as swift as his poor fatigued heart may permit to the *Commissariat de Police*. Nothing is known. They promise to make immediate search – but where? Ah indeed, where? At home again, exhausted with these emotions, sleep overcomes us, momentarily, only a minute. And in that minute there is a bang at the door – it is *en effet* the bang that awakes us – we leap to our feet, fly to the threshold and what do we there see? Our Miriam! She is speechless, sitting, her head against the lintel!'

'Madame Z!' I exclaimed. 'What a terrible story!'

'Worse is to come, monsieur.' Madame Z. had recovered her poise by now. Anger, I think. 'She is *ivre morte*!'

Dead drunk? Miriam? Miriam on a jag?

Madame Z. resumed her tale. 'I am obliged to recount these cruel details, monsieur, for without them your task will be still more difficult. Attend, please.'

There was not much more to hear. It seems that by the time all the neighbours were out of bed and assembled – for it was already half-past two in the morning – Miriam had been taken into her home, she had been cajoled, her cheeks had been slapped to bring her to her senses, feathers had been burnt under her nose with no result at all, and then someone had divulged that a foreign voice had been heard in the alley at about the time of her return, a man's voice, mumbling and influenced by drink.

'Foreign. You have noted the fact, monsieur? No doubt American or English. And . . . '

'What do you wish me to do then, madame?'

She looked quite surprised. 'But naturally! Find the man! *Cherchez le monstre qui a . . .* '

'I suppose there is no doubt, madame, that someone has . . . Forgive me but . . . '

'Doubt? Pray forgive *me*, but who could be in doubt? Moreover it is one of your countrymen and I request you to find him so that though all is lost, honour at least may be saved.'

'And the police, madame? Are they not working on this tragedy?'

'Everyone is required to help, monsieur.'

* * *

And the sequel. I learnt it this morning with relief which was almost as profound as Madame Z.'s.

Under the salts – whatever they were – or possibly because the drink fumes had dissipated themselves as the hours passed, Miriam revived. She did not doubt either that the worst had befallen when they told her what I have just recorded. It would be a terrible blow to any girl; to Miriam, it was the most terrible. She was courageous and, by dipping into her memory, she was able to recall what had happened and how, though she had the delicacy not to speak of it. However, she was compelled to divulge some part of the truth – that she had yielded to an invitation pressed upon her by a stranger – yes, a foreigner, and handsome – because in the course of the day, a witness came forward to report having seen Miriam with this person as they were about to buy provisions for a little supper.

The doors of the Z. home were closed, with only the most intimate of neighbours admitted to the family council. After some hours of discussion, one of the neighbours said, 'And have you consulted a wise-woman, Madame Z?'

'It is scarcely necessary to do so, madame,' was the reply.

'Yet, is there not a possibility that no *lasting* harm . . . ?'

'No possibility, madame, nevertheless . . . '

So a wise-woman was consulted. She and Madame Z. and the reluctant Miriam were locked away in the inner of the two rooms, leaving the neighbours to listen at the door. They had not long to wait.

'Madame,' came the wise-woman's voice after a while, evidently addressing Madame Z., 'though it is true that even now I cannot assure you that Mademoiselle is no longer chaste, it is also true that I cannot be sure she is still chaste without question. All I can guarantee is that if you will have the goodness to use a medicament of which I alone know the secret, no one will henceforth be in the position to tell the difference.' And with this she must have produced a phial or a box or a screw of paper containing the secret medicament.

'Come, child,' the wise-woman's voice went on, 'let me explain . . . ' She lowered her voice to a whisper and explained.

Suddenly, in the midst of these whisperings, Miriam's voice rang out loud, clear and triumphant.

'I *see*! Then I am a virgin . . . I am a virgin!'

It was a little miracle. Miriam, well brought-up as she had been, had not presumed to interrupt the wise-woman earlier, but now for the first time, whatever her girlish uncertainties had been before, she knew exactly how it comes about that all maidens start chaste but some do not remain so. All these years she had relied upon her conscience to tell her, and her conscience – though not perhaps entirely clear on what had happened the previous night – was now clear enough to enable her to run to the door, fling it open and cry to the assembled neighbours, 'I am a virgin, I am a virgin!' She then sped into the alley to tell all those who did not already know.

Everybody knows now, of course – at least everybody in the Mellah or who passes up and down the street in which Miriam plies her Pfaff. Madame Z. herself encouraged the spreading of the news as widely as possible; naturally, because only a few hours before she had been leading them to believe precisely to the contrary.

She paid me a special visit to tell me. 'Providence is after all very merciful,' she finished up. 'Nevertheless I am obliged to punish Miriam for her foolhardiness, since Providence did not.'

* * *

The alley off Riad ez-Zitoun is very pleasant, but I miss the earthiness of Derb esh-Shems. Here my neighbours are of grander stock, though not grand – moderately successful merchants' families and the like. They give me a dignified greeting when we meet but I don't believe they will ever be as much part of my life as the others were.

My house is like a little island here, whereas in Derb esh-Shems it seemed that it was just a room leading off a corridor, and the corridor, the street. However, Riad ez-Zitoun is much more peaceful, and I bless Madame T. for leaving me in charge of it.

* * *

I ran into Idrees and Moulay Yacoub last night. They have paid me a formal visit at Riad ez-Zitoun, just to look, but we normally meet outdoors. I found them on the road-level terrace of the Café de France; they were drinking coffee together. On my way in to the bar, I stopped to talk to them for a moment.

'Come in and have a "Stork" or something,' I suggested. 'Stork' is a beer made in Casablanca. I know Moulay Yacoub never drinks, because he had told me so, but I suspected Idrees would like a beer, though not in full view of the passers-by on the terrace. Stimulants are forbidden by the Qoran and, as a matter of fact, a *Dahir* – a proclamation of the

Sultan – specifically forbids the sale of alcoholic drinks to Moorish muslims. The *Dahir* hangs framed on the walls of all licensed premises, but, sensibly enough, official eyes are generally closed to reasonable contraventions of it.

'*Tch, tch!* I do not take beer,' Idrees said. '*Very* bad.'

'And *hashshish*, Idrees? Is that good?'

'I do not take *hashshish. Tch.*'

'Anyway I'm going in. Perhaps I'll see you later.' I turned to go in and caught sight of a Moulay we all know, happily sipping a *rosé* at the bar-counter. 'Look, Idrees! There's a Moulay drinking *rosé*! So it's all right.'

'No,' Moulay Yacoub said. 'And he is a Moulay.'

'Moulays' are of course descendants of the family of the Prophet Mohammed and in a sense not only superior persons but also privileged. A Moulay is described as '*sharif*' – noble. Seigneur Hamed whom I had met in Tangier was noble in this sense, though I did not realize it at the time.

'Are Moulays allowed to drink *rosé*, then?'

'No.'

'Then I don't know what you mean, Moulay Yacoub.'

'It is quite different. Moulays are noble.'

It was wrong of me to tease him on a subject of this kind, but I did. I said: 'I think that if a Moulay takes the advantages of his nobility, he should also accept the disadvantages. He should be an example to others who are not noble.'

'Why?'

'Well, that's what I think. Perhaps English people feel that way. For instance, in England we have a Queen and you may believe that she has advantages over the rest of us. She has in a way – she doesn't go hungry or thirsty, she lives in palaces. But our Queen, whom we love in a very strange and very deep fashion, cannot at all do as she pleases. She is less free than the smallest of her subjects. She is noble.'

'It is quite different,' Moulay Yacoub said. 'I agree that your Queen is noble, but in another fashion. She is not of the family of the Prophet Mohammed, on whom be peace.'

Idrees nodded and said, 'You understand? Moulay is very *spécial*.'

'We think our Queen is *spécial*, too.'

'We too will honour your Queen, but we cannot think that she is *lalla, une sharīfa*, because she is not of the family.'

After all, fundamentally it is the same thing – a mystical aristocracy. We in England focus the sum total of our acceptance on one being, the Monarch, the Defender of the Faith. The Muslims find nothing strange about a diffusion of a similar acceptance throughout the multitudes of nobles descended from the Prophet of Allah. So I apologized to them.

'I believe we are both right – these are things inside us, having no need of words.'

'*Vive le roi!*' said Moulay Yacoub.

So I went into the bar, leaving them to their coffee.

The days have been growing shorter and there is a chill in the air after sundown, with the result that the inner bars of cafés do more business. Hitherto it has been the road-level terraces that have been crowded. Now it is the bars, and they have a good many Moorish clients. The atmosphere varies from day to day. Generally the Moors seem quite unaware of sinning, but sometimes they run in, gulp down two or three quick ones and scuttle out again. This is on evenings when news comes over the grapevine that the authorities have decided to use their powers for some reason or another. Last night was a placid night.

Moors don't hold their drink well. They drink too fast, in the first place. I must record, however, that even at their most boisterous they are nearly always good-humoured, and this is a remarkable testimony to the Moroccan character. They behave nicely as a rule, partly because that is their nature and partly, without doubt, because if they don't the barman will refuse to serve them. With that framed *Dahir* on the wall behind him he has power to do as he pleases. So clients smile sweetly at him and behave, more or less. I give the authorities and the café-patrons full marks for allowing what they cannot in any case prevent, and for controlling the situation so neatly.

* * *

At last I have a new servant and, oddly enough, it was the least likely of the friends who had kindly agreed to help who has produced her for me – Haroon. I opened my door to someone's knocking and there was Haroon with a small, fat, elderly Moorish woman whom he introduced as 'Fatima'.

Haroon went away singing, with a tip in his pocket, and Fatima and I stood looking each other over. Under her veil, her face is wrinkled like a soft walnut.

* * *

Americans have been pouring into the district to work on a big construction job some distance from Marrakesh. They mostly seem to be boys who have not travelled a great deal, and they are easy prey for the guides when they come in to town. Of course, as soon as they discover that they are being made to pay too much for whatever they buy or do, they get surly and make '*ennuis*' for everyone concerned, but Haroon is pleased with them and thinks he will reap some of the profits.

All during the week these Americans are kept busy at their work, but on Saturdays they come to town to let their hair down. Then the Café de France is full of them, wearing clothes that modern-minded Moors get very excited about. They appear nice and friendly, but when they get drunk they believe they ought to fight. Why, I don't know. Quite old men are sometimes to be seen putting their spectacles away and preparing to jump on each other. This much astonishes the Moors, but they are inclined to like the visitors because they are so ready to be led round the sights and don't really involve Marrakeshis in their '*ennuis*' and battles.

The start of this construction job has meant vacancies for labour, so there has been a great rush for jobs, manual jobs mostly, for which Moors are being recruited at pay many times greater than local Marrakesh rates. A certain kind of Moor cannot resist this, even though it means getting up at four each morning, travelling by train as near as the rail goes to their destination, and thence in something rather sombrely called a 'man-lift' for the last few kilometres. They get back home at about eight o'clock in the evening, so probably they earn every franc they get. At the weekends, these Moors are to be seen promenading the streets with American boys. Communication is almost impossible between them for want of a common language, but each side gets something out of it, I dare say, and the ladies in the *quartier réservé* are delighted. So delighted are they that they readily grant expensive favours to the Moors who have shown the boys the way.

It's hard for these American boys. There are no girls for them to 'date' in this town – only girls who expect to be paid and left to get on with their evening's waiting-list, and the boys have no armour against such a system. They look bewildered and unhappy, and perhaps that's why they get drunk and release their unhappiness in street fights. It's a circle, but not vicious at all. Marrakesh must seem a very one-horse town to them.

There are, of course, some amongst this growing community of Americans who have been around a good deal, and have perhaps learned a foreign language into the bargain. I know two such – Bob and Dave. They're happy enough, because they don't expect life here to follow the American pattern. They have rented a little house in the city for weekends, made themselves as comfortable as local resources permit and have even managed to get a little bit under the skin of Marrakeshi life. I met Bob first in a bar, and since then have been to their house two or three times. I like them very much. They both know the English pretty well, but some things puzzle, even embarrass, them. For example, we were talking the other day about an Englishman I know slightly who is a local-hire man at the American camp. In commenting on this man's readiness to work hard for a fraction of the pay an American received for the same job, I had said that I understood his family had been rather well-to-do in the past.

'Listen here, Peter,' Bob said, 'don't get me wrong, but when Englishmen say that, we Americans get an uncomfortable feeling right here.'

'What do you mean? I don't follow?'

'Well, nearly every Englishman I meet seems to have glories in his personal past he'd be glad to have me know about. But we don't look at it that way; we look at the present, or the future. I wouldn't want you to misunderstand me, but isn't it just a little symptomatic?'

It is indeed symptomatic. I think it must be even more tiresome than boasting about the present.

*　*　*

Bou Djem'a, the negro I met so long ago at 'Aysha's *dyufa*, came running after me and made such a to-do about where I had been all this while, and why had I not constantly visited him at his house, that I invited him, and the two friends who were taking the air of the Djema'a el-Fna with him, back to Riad ez-Zitoun for a chat, and perhaps an aperitif. They consulted each other in whispers and then said they would like to come.

We sat talking in the patio for an hour or so and finished what was left of a Cinzano bottle, and it was quite a pleasant little interlude. Bou Djem'a then said to one of his two friends, and pointing at me, 'Mohamed, this gentleman is *écrivain* – a writer.'

'Are you *écrivain?*' Mohamed asked and Bou Djem'a answered for me, 'Yes.'

'*El-hamdu l-llah!* God be praised!' Mohamed said. 'Can you write French?'

I said yes, I could.

'In that case you will please write a letter for me. I will come tomorrow, *Insha'Allah*, at the one-and-a-half. You will be here? You have paper and envelope? And stamps?'

I have not been asked for a service of this kind for quite a while now. 'Of course. But come at twelve, or twelve-thirty,' I said.

'I cannot come at the twelve-and-a-half. Tomorrow is Friday It will be nearing mosque-time. I will come at the one-and-a-half,' I said.

'In that case,' I said, 'you had better come to lunch. Bou Djem'a? Will you come too? And your other friend?'

Again they consulted together, and agreed that they would all three come, *Insha'Allah*. They left soon after, and that was that.

That was yesterday. Accordingly, I trotted off to the market this morning to get what was necessary for lunch. Fatima is doing all right, and is quite capable of buying for a Moorish dish, but this time I thought it might be amusing to try an Indian curry with pilaf. There is a recipe for curried chicken on the cover of a tin of Venkatachellum's curry powder in Madame T.'s kitchen. It would be suitably hot and spiced for Moorish palates and a change from the eternal *tajīn* of beef. So I spent a lot of time choosing ingredients and improvising where the proper materials were absent. And then I prepared everything myself, because Fatima isn't much good on these occasions. She knows what she has to do but she doesn't seem able to decide upon the order in which the tasks should be done. It can happen (it does happen) that whereas she has completed the household wash and perhaps done some sock-mending by midday, she has not managed to get down to preparing lunch. Anyway I cooked the lunch today – and I alone ate it. Fatima had gone off for her Friday afternoon *hammām* and my three guests simply did not turn up. I was very annoyed, but resigned.

This afternoon, about three o'clock when I was on my way to visit Maurice, I was a great deal more annoyed and less resigned to see Bou Djem'a and his two friends sitting outside a coffee-stall.

'*Lā bās!*' Bou Djem'a called out to me in greeting. '*Kull shay lā bās?*'

'What happened?' I asked, as calmly as I could manage.

'*Kifāsh?* Oh yes . . . We became engaged, you see, me and my friends. Never mind. We will come to lunch with you some other day, *Insha'Allah.*'

'Some other day,' Mohamed said. 'And also the letter.'

'Sit and take coffee,' the third said.

I sat and had coffee, because I understand now.

* * *

This is what I understand now and have failed to understand hitherto.

Insha' Allah is very important. I have known that for a long time. But having uttered the formula *Insha' Allah* – if God wills – it is the next step that troubles the Western mind, though it troubles mine no longer. What actually happens?

Well, what happens depends upon whether you need to do the thing referred to, whether your comfort or livelihood depend upon it. If the thing has no importance – which is taken to mean that it has no real bearing upon your personal prosperity or pleasure – you may quite easily find that something outside your control prevents your doing whatever it was. For example, perhaps on the way to this engagement, you meet a friend and the friend is thirsty and needs mint tea. He obliges you to sit with him in a tea shop. Or something else unforeseeable happens. Anyway, there it is, the appointment has been missed. The person with whom the appointment has been made will perfectly understand the innumerable ways you may have been prevented from keeping it. It is likely that he too, poor fellow, has been prevented in one or other of these ways, so that there will be no one at the rendezvous at all.

Naturally, you have to agree at the time to whatever is suggested, *Insha' Allah*, for it would be exceedingly rude to say 'no' to anything. Yet to agree certainly smacks of presumption, of an attempt to interfere with the workings of fate. The past is past; the present is living evidence of God's wishes, but the future is in His hands. How can you foretell what He has in mind for you when you are making your plans? Anyone can see that the very fact of failure to carry out such plans shows that He never intended that you should.

I have worked this out for myself. No Moor would agree that it was an accurate explanantion, but it satisfies me without in the least affecting my fondness for these people. It is no good fighting against Fate or facts.

* * *

Fatima arrived with a chicken this morning, very pleased with herself. 'It was presented to me by my nephew,' she announced, 'I shall make of it *couscous*.'

It was a nice plump little chicken and I thanked her. 'We shall have it for lunch and I shall invite Monsieur Maurice to eat it too.'

Fatima likes Maurice.

I had the idea that we might stuff it with the pilaf rice I had made for the curry yesterday, of which there was a great deal left over. So I led Fatima to the ice-box and explained what I wanted her to do.

I think she was angry because she had wanted *couscous*, that dull thing they make with semolina. So she pretended not to understand. 'What? How?'

I said: 'Well, just put the rice in it. Stuff the little chicken with the rice. Look, the rice has almonds and raisins and many good things in it, already cooked.'

'I don't know anything.' This is what she always seems to say when I ask the impossible of her. Anything is impossible that she does not want to do, or know how to do already.

'Come now, it's easy.'

'How?'

My Arabic is certainly improving – it has just had to improve or I should get nowhere, but it is still somewhat limited. Not surprisingly, I lack cooking terms, so I had to improvise.

'Well, it isn't at all difficult. The pilaf is cooked and spiced. Push it into the chicken.'

She looked at me sullenly. 'Where?'

'Into its . . . ' and I used the only term I know.

Imagine my horror to find Fatima, her hands clasped over her eyes, swaying about the kitchen! What had come over her? Her whole body was shaking with emotion. Emotion? Or could it be laughter? It was uncontrollable laughter. She sank on to her knees and heaved about in the middle of the floor. Then she peeped out at me, and I could see that her face was convulsed. She tried to say the word, but couldn't and she exploded again.

'*Khalli-ni, khalli-ni* . . . !' she moaned. 'Leave me! Oh m'soo, m'soo . . . ' Then she rallied for a moment, sighing. 'Leave me! *Ghadi nekhemmem-'aleyh*. I shall think about it.'

The chicken was perfect, and Maurice even congratulated Fatima upon its cooking. She turned and raced from the room, her hand over her mouth, and we could hear her struggling for breath in the kitchen next door.

* * *

I witnessed something yesterday evening which would have shocked me in the past. Perhaps it does even now, a little. It was about sunset on the Djema'a el-Fna and the *place* was of course crowded. I had come across 'Abdeslem and we were strolling together, and chatting. Naturally, he was telling me about himself, and about 'Aysha incidentally, filling in the gaps of my knowledge since I moved to Riad ez-Zitoun. I haven't seen 'Aysha at all since then. Once I went to Derb esh-Shems to call on her, but the door was locked.

'She is well and strong,' 'Abdeslem was saying, 'because she battens upon me. See how thin and sick I have become.'

'You were worse when you were bewitched, 'Abdeslem.'

'That? Ah yes. *'Andek-el-haqq*. I was even worse. You do not think I am sick now? I wish to sleep for the winter like such animals as . . . as . . . '

'Tortoises?' I suggested.

'Perhaps . . . ' but his mind was suddenly on something else, a couple of girls in *djellabas*, scuttling about the *place*, peeping, or trying to peep, over the shoulders of the men grouped round the various mountebanks, rolling their eyes above the little embroidered veils they wore. 'Abdeslem made a loud cough and a kissing noise. Then he said '*ssss!*'

I have no concern with 'Abdeslem's morals, but it did seem a little risky for him to be manuring his plans on the open *place* with who knew which of 'Aysha's acquaintances looking on. 'Aysha is rather ruthless, after all, and I imagine she regards 'Abdeslem as hers by right of conquest. I said something of the kind to him.

'Who fears 'Aysha?' he asked.

The two girls looked uncertainly at him, whispered together and then hurried away. 'Abdeslem caught me by the arm and pulled me along after them. They hadn't gone far, of course. They were standing in a little group, watching a curious, old bearded man, a doctor of some sort, who is considered a great specialist in stomach pains; almost any pains, I think, but stomach particularly.

'They are from the *quartier réservé*,' Abdeslem hissed at me, leading me alongside the girls; I suppose in order to further his suit. I tried to see what the old bearded man was up to. He had a couple of knives heating on a brazier and a man beside him on the asphalt, with his shirt held up to bare his stomach. The old man picked up a knife, spat on it as a laundress spits on an iron to test its heat and, being satisfied with the sharp hiss it gave out, picked up a pinch of greyish powder and put it on his tongue. Then, muttering a brief prayer, he suddenly passed the almost red-hot knife across his tongue. We all gasped, his tongue hissed like an iron, and thereupon he made a dive for the poor wretch's stomach and proceeded to spread the powder over it as if his tongue were a spatula. Then he massaged the stomach and it was at once cured. The man said so. Someone else was taking the patient's place. I was staring in horrified fascination, but shouts and a sharp blow in the ribs brought me swinging round towards 'Abdeslem.

Two of the Pasha's police – they are distinct from the official French-controlled police force – had seized the two girls. The girls screamed – everyone screams or shouts when something like this happens – but the police didn't care: they dragged the girls away. The girls struggled and kicked, but the men simply took a firmer hold and lugged them off like animals to the slaughterhouse. It was not so much this that shocked me, because, after all, there is a well-organized *quartier réservé* where the girls can do as they please and it is therefore quite right that they should be prevented from conducting their *commerce* on the public streets. I was shocked by the reaction of the men, including 'Abdeslem. I think the men were delighted, and I think their delight derives from a deep-rooted fear of their womenfolk. The women are exceedingly tough. It is true that they submit to being incarcerated in their homes, or in the *quartier réservé* if they are those kind of girls, but they are the masters all right. It is not only 'Aysha who is ruthless. Moors use their women, or believe that they use them, but in reality all commerce with women, even with wives, is fraught with danger for the men. Men are put under spells, poisoned, driven mad, sucked dry of life. I am afraid that this is undoubtedly true, and an exhibition such as I witnessed yesterday evening seems to offer the promise of revenge – some evidence of the worm turning. The men laughed exultantly as the two girls were dragged away to be imprisoned or pay a fine, and probably to be beaten a little too.

'Did you see?' 'Abdeslem asked in triumph.

It's no good trying to judge by Western standards – they don't fit.

* * *

Haroon has been dejected recently because he does not seem to be making much progress with the Americans after all. They are kind to him, and they give him a cigarette sometimes, but not one of them has agreed to employ him as a guide. The reasons are clear enough, though not clear to poor little Haroon: he lacks even so much as a few words of English and his legs are too short to keep pace with those whose legs are of normal length. Moreover, he suspects that he does not appear 'serious', so for some time he has been in a dejected mood. Today, however, he is a changed being. I found him perched in front of a table at the Café de France, where tourists might see him. He had a pencil in his hand.

He looked up self-importantly and said, 'Do you know what I am now doing? I am drawing pictures. Look!'

He had drawn several – of animals and men and women, distinguishable the one from the other by the number of their legs and Haroon's symbols for their sex. They were very funny indeed.

'What are you going to do with them, Haroon?'

'Do? Why, sell them, of course. To the tourists.'

'Have you sold any?'

'Not yet. I must colour them first, you understand. But I have no colours to colour them with. Do you think that you could help me to find colours?' he asked tentatively.

I said that I would.

'It's easy to draw,' Haroon remarked. 'Easier than being a guide. What shall I now draw?'

'Some more of those things, I think,' I told him. 'They ought to sell nicely, but don't let the police catch you, because you're not really supposed to draw them.'

'Because I'm Muslim?'

Orthodox Muslims are prohibited from drawing or in any way representing the human form, though this is not what I had in mind.

'No, not because you're a Muslim. Because . . . ' But after all, why should I expect Haroon to submit to Western tyranny? So I said, 'I don't know why not, really.'

'Do you think that's a nice one?' he asked me, looking up from his sketch.

Some Moors draw and paint, and some have a naïvely charming little talent and a very few something more than that. And, oddly enough, of the drawings I have seen, nearly all have been the work of domestic servants employed by Europeans who have encouraged them. Two or three Moorish painters of 'primitives' have rightly made both money and little reputations for themselves. Why should not Haroon cash in on it, if he could? He certainly had a very bold approach.

* * *

A Moorish woman was walking ahead of me and, when she came to it, turned into my alley. I followed, because that was the way I was going. She was dressed in a cream gabardine *djellaba* and stumped along on wedge-soled shoes. The shoes were of pink plastic, and too tight, I fancy. I thought I recognized the brooch with which she had pinned back her *djellaba* hood – a Pierrot's head in gilt, with red glass eyes – but my mind was on other things, and it was only when I saw that she was making for my door that I knew who it was. 'Aysha, of course.

''Aysha!' I called, and she turned round.

'*El-hamdu l-llah! Voici la troisième fois que je te rends visite!* Three times in three days, *voyons*, and three times you are not there! Where do you go in the afternoon at this hour? I have something very important to say to you, Monsieur Peter.'

'Come in, then, 'Aysha. Would you like some tea? We can make some. The servant goes after lunch.'

'Servant? Yes, I had heard. You have become very chic.' But she declined tea, being unwilling to cause me trouble, she said. However, she agreed to accept a glass of vermouth, in order to be amiable to me.

'And now, in the European fashion, I will tell you my purpose. No polite delays between you and me, Monsieur Peter, *n'est-ce pas?*'

'Yes. Tell me what it is. And why have you not visited me here long before?' Abdeslem has been. Why have not you?'

'Mm–m . . . 'Abdeslem. But first let me speak of the matter which is in my heart. I wish you, Monsieur Peter, to bring me to the Café de France.'

Maybe it is a long time since I have seen 'Aysha, but not so long that I should forget that her mind is capable of twistings and turnings which obscure the true direction. 'The Café de France? I have never seen you there, 'Aysha.'

'Moorish ladies are not accustomed to go there, as you must know.'

She understands the technique of playing for time, in others as well as in herself. 'To the Café de la Splendeur, yes, at a latish hour if in the company of a gentleman. But to the Café de France Moorish ladies do not go at all, even with gentlemen.'

'That makes it difficult, of course. I can see that.'

'It would be of no difficulty – even of the most *minuscule* – for *you*, Monsieur Peter. For you are as one of the little marble tables on the *terrasse* of that elegant café – for ever there, and respected now by the patron and *garçons* alike.'

'Now? Was I not respected before, then?'

'Who will respect a foreigner unknown? But *now*, known and loved . . . ' She smiled flatteringly. '*You* may do as your heart pleases in the Café de France.'

'Good. And why do you wish to go there?'

'Ah . . . I have reasons. Reasons of great interest, and therefore you must help me.'

She paused again, waiting for my reactions. I tried to show none, because I still did not know what she was getting at. 'I can't think what these reasons may be,' I said at last. 'You are not after all greatly attached to aperitifs, I think, and . . . '

'*Au contraire*, I am *excessivement* attached, but that is not the question. Yet you might have the goodness to pour me a second little glass. *Merci*. As we say – *Baraka llahu f ik.*' She paused yet again. 'The climate turns sultry, hm–m . . . ?'

'No. I don't find it so. Perhaps you would like to take off your *djellaba*?' She was fanning herself with a lace handkerchief. She had already taken off her veil in order to drink. The veil lay on her lap, a little chiffon thing with a chain-stitch pattern of roses on it.

'No. *Ough!* There is no air in your house.' She took off her shoes and I saw the relief come into her eyes.

'Now won't you tell me what remains hidden in your heart, 'Aysha?'

She pretended not to have heard. Instead, as she allowed her gaze to travel slowly about the room, she said, 'Now, *par exemple*, those *Americán* . . . the town is full on Saturday. Everywhere they are, large, kind, generous men and rich.' For a second her beady, black eyes lit on me and then flicked away again.

'Today chances to be Saturday, does it not?' I asked. I had suddenly realized the purpose of all these fine clothes and phrases.

'*Peut-être* . . .' she murmured politely. 'Ah, yes. Yesterday *l-hammām*, thus today is Saturday . . .'

'And you are perhaps thinking that these Americans, tired from the labours of their week, may have earned a moment of leisure?'

'I am grieved for those *Américán, et c'est la vérité*.'

'It is a hard life they lead, but they are well paid for it.'

'I am grieved,' 'Aysha resumed in a firm voice, 'because I have heard that ladies without scruples take their *portefeuilles* from them while they repose themselves. I am ashamed for women, Monsieur Peter. *En effet*, I am wondering how, *how* I can help – should I not, for example, offer asylum at the weekends to one or more of these *pauvres garçons*?'

Now that the truth had begun to wriggle into the open, 'Aysha found less difficulty in revealing it. 'So, Monsieur Peter,' she continued self-confidently, 'you will accompany me to the Café de France. Between friends it is nothing to visit the bar of that café – particularly when *one* of the two friends has already served the *other* with a kindness, yes?'

'Naturally I understand, on principle, but to what kindness are you referring, I ask myself – '

'To a kindness concerning a *fiancée*, for instance, without which an *ennui* was ensuing . . . Between friends such kindnesses are impossible to forget, I believe, and further I add that a visit to the bar is so simple a thing – one visits the bar, one offers the lady an aperitif in the *bar* (*not* the terrace, the *bar*), and perhaps for amiability one also invites such gentlemen alone that may be here and there at the bar, as it might be a lonely *Américán*, or even two – one invites such to drink a glass with one in the name of *relations internationales*.' She stopped to draw breath and look at me.

'The bar – not the terrace – I understand. I don't think the patron will admit ladies like – well, like . . . Anyway, he does not admit ladies to the bar in the ordinary way, I mean . . .'

She waved the obstruction aside. 'That is why you must accompany. To proceed. When the stranger should chance to be *Americán*, a problem poses itself.' She put out the tip of her tongue and tapped it. '*La langue, ti comprends?* The *Americán* language. But you speak it, naturally.'

'I see. You wish me to bring you into a circle of friendship with such poor lonely Americans and also to act as *homme de confiance et interprète*. That is it, is it not?'

She smiled gratefully. 'Exactly! You have understood. How could I ever have doubted it? First, I had thought to beg of you to teach me the tongue, then I feared that such a matter would take too long, and each week wasted is a week thus wasted. Then, as I was on the road to your house, this fine solution presented itself to me. I am deeply *reconnaissante, cher monsieur*.'

'But you know, 'Aysha, much as I love and respect you, and grateful as I am for your help in matters now mercifully past, I do not think I can do as you ask of me.'

'And why not? Other gentlemen do it for ladies each weekend – and for ladies so unworthy it is an *honte*, and . . . '

'That is another matter.'

'It is the *same* matter and you are the only gentleman for me. Do you not understand? Come! Let us waste no more time. Already the bar of the Café de France will be full of these poor lonely boys. And what I should prefer,' she went on, rising to examine herself in a mirror and to adjust her veil, 'would be to choose a gentleman who searches for a *fiancée* for all the weekends of his visit to Morocco. *Ti comprends?*'

'And what about 'Abdeslem?'

'My shoes, if you please, *cher monsieur. Merci*. 'Abdeslem? It is the needs of 'Abdeslem that are always in my mind. *Hélas*, he says he is unable to work his charcoal *commerce* because of his debilities, and one cannot allow the dear *garçon* to starve. That is yet another reason to give assistance to your friends, as you can see. Money is required.'

'I see. Then if 'Abdeslem approves of the solution, why does he not himself accompany you to the Café de France, 'Aysha?'

'Because, *idiot* – forgive me – 'Abdeslem does not speak the *Americán* language nor can he approve of alcohol. That is why, and fine reasons both.' Having dealt with my objections, she set herself to examine my clothes. 'You are aware that these *Americán* are very splendidly clad? I think it will be correct for you to put on a *costume* for this visit, do you not?'

It was time to stand firm.

'I cannot accompany you. I very much regret it, but it is impossible for me. Just as 'Abdeslem cannot approve of alcohol, so, amongst my people, it would be considered bad to do as you propose. Very stupid, no doubt, but that is the case.'

Her lips compressed themselves into little bloodless ridges. 'Mm-m. I am unable to see how it is bad. You are assisting friends, is it not? Two friends – me and 'Abdeslem, *yak*? And if it is bad, then you intend to say that such bad things as you wish to do you *will* do, and such bad things as you do *not* wish to do, you will *not* do? And while you behave in this wicked manner, your friends may die of hunger and thirst?'

'I'm very sorry, 'Aysha. I would like to help, but this I cannot do.'

'I understand now,' she said after a moment. She nodded self-righteously as she pulled the hood of her *djellaba* forward over her head. 'It is that all men are *hlālef* – *cochons. Comment dis-tu "cochon" en anglais?*'

'Pig.'

She picked up her little bag and started towards the door, and then turned to face me. 'Peeg, peeg, peeg!' she shouted. '*Je te laisse* – I leave you to the terrible things that peegs will do! I shall not wish to meet you again thereafter!'

Maurice's *commerce* seems to have got away to a good start. He is naturally pleased, and particularly pleased because he has been proved right on the subject of casual tourists and 'teas'.

'They come and they sit and it may appear that they desire nothing but to repose their feet,' Maurice says, 'and then the major-domo enters, charms them with *thé à la menthe*, keeps them waiting for the change at the entrance to the *boutique de souvenirs* on the first floor; they are tempted, they buy some objects, and everyone is contented.'

It is quite true. I have seen it happening. The major-domo is a success, tall and dignified, slow moving, with the air of a chamberlain who receives honoured guests of the house. There is an atmosphere of quiet and repose – no wonder the clients are glad to take the weight off their poor feet and rest for a while in one of the *salons* on the top floor.

The *salons* seem part of a private house. There is nothing that is not for sale (except perhaps the divans), yet nothing that does not appear to be part of a beautiful and lived-in room.

Today when I went round I found Maurice setting up a banana tree in one of the vestibules.

'I have been obliged to cut it down because of changes in the garden,' he explained. He was arranging it in a room too low for it, so that its long, cool leaves spread themselves into a green tent. An enormous purple-red banana flower hung like a lantern from the ceiling.

The pavilion is filled with plants, and a family of sparrows has set up house in one of the rooms. Through a window I could see a group of clients coming through the orchard.

'Look! Clients.'

'Then let us go away.' He quickly led me to an exit, abandoning the *bananier*. It is not that he does not wish to meet the clients, rather that he thinks they prefer to be left alone. We walked under the fruit trees to the end of the orchard, where he is building a small cottage which he plans to occupy himself later on. It is very small, no more than two rooms and a little bathroom. One of the rooms already existed before, built into the masonry of the thick *riad* wall. He showed me how work was progressing. The reorganization of the old room is nearly complete. He does not intend to fit modern plumbing because he prefers the Eastern method.

'I have received a letter from Madame T.,' he said. 'It concerns you also. She is returning to Marrakesh earlier than she had expected. She hopes that this fact will not too much incommode you.'

* * *

I always knew that Madame T. intended to come back in the spring and that there was a possibility of her affairs allowing her to return earlier. It is evident from her letter that she will be here again by Christmas.

This news came sharply into focus when I was at the post office collecting my mail today and my eye lit upon their calendar. It is already the 28th of November. In less than a month I must move out of Riad ez-Zitoun. Of course, I can't return to Derb esh-Shems.

The influx of Americans has not only affected weekend trade at the Café de France, it has also caused house rents to rise steeply. Of course Americans who want houses or apartments want them in the *ville nouvelle*, where modern plumbing and other conveniences they consider essential are available. But house-owners in the old city, where nothing of that kind exists, have raised rents on principle. I know this from Idrees the *simsar*. Idrees is doubly disturbed by it. While this situation lasts, no one wishes to sell because he dreams of a fortune from rents and, on the other hand, no one is prepared to take a *medina* house on rent at the current artificial price levels. For me, the news of Madame T.'s. unexpectedly early return is also a shock. I have to start thinking about money again long before I had intended to.

The position is that my funds in Moroccan or French francs will be running out soon, even if I contrive to live very cheaply, and the only way I can see of replenishing them is not only to finish the novel but also to find an American publisher. Dollars can be remitted to Morocco; sterling cannot. In a vague sort of way, Madame T.'s return in the spring represents a D-day decision for me. I must find a little house to rent at a price I can afford, or revert to some kind of hotel – or go. I cannot bear to think of going. There is another *ennui* too, though it is a minor one. A very good friend of mine, an Englishman, will be visiting Marrakesh after Christmas. He is a man whose hospitality I have often enjoyed elsewhere, and I had offered him a bed in Riad ez-Zitoun and the sort of food Fatima tosses together in her *tajīn*. He does not need my hospitality, but I very much want to impose it upon him. It now looks as if he will escape the threat.

*   *   *

This boring problem of economics compels me to consider relinquishing Fatima. She has a home and rich relatives who can feed her, so that a month's saving of her wages and the food she eats at my expense represent more to me at the moment than their loss would to her. I have told her what is in my mind and there have been terrible dramas over it. Never before has she shown the least indication of enjoying her work or of liking me, but now she says that she will never leave me; that even if I don't pay her she will remain with me always, and that no doubt God will provide. This is all very well, but it means that God must provide for me so that I can provide for both of us – because obviously there is no real question of her working for nothing. We argued about it and shouted at each other much of the morning and I sipped 'Old Lady's Gin' to reinforce my determination, and suddenly, after quite a lot of gin, it occurred to me that perhaps Fatima could paint pictures and sell them like other people's servants. I asked and she said no. But when I gave her a piece of paper and some charcoal, she drew beautifully, or so it seemed to me. It was as if I had thrown the baby into the ocean and the little mite had astonished me by performing an instinctive breaststroke to land.

I have now pinned half a dozen sheets of paper to the pastry-board and left Fatima with orders to cover them all with whatever she fancies, and that she is not to leave the kitchen before she has done so. By this time she was giggling, and quite excited by the game.

* * *

The ridiculous thing is that Fatima's drawings, which she has now coloured as well, look to me quite as good as some of the stuff I have seen exhibited. In fact, I enjoy the pleasant feeling of having invented something. Of course, I have done it with the worst possible intentions, for if we can sell anything I shall take a commission out of which I shall pay her salary and for our food. Anyway, I have said we shall try – housework in the mornings and 'art' in the afternoons. She laughed like a child and said '*Wakhkha*'.

* * *

Magic shows signs of giving way to medical science on the Djema'a el-Fna, but slowly – because magic has deep roots and science is – let's face it – so very improbable. Anyone can see why the application of lion fat should be so strengthening – though there are no lions hereabouts and consequently no indigenous fat, and elephants (which might do instead) have been unknown in Morocco since about AD 400, according to *Michelin*. The

Moors, however, feel about certain guanas and lizardy things much as they might feel about lions: they are known to be very helpful in various types of trouble. And then there are things of a particular shape or smell, or colour or consistency, that by their very nature restore the failing principles of life. And there are certain other ugly things which, if need be, cool the blood. Of course, the things themselves have to be carefully prepared, and their preparation is apt to change their appearance, so that the way to present them for sale is to lay the extracts or essences out on the cobbles, alongside recognizable parts of the creature or plant to which they belonged. But science is different. How can you perceive the virtue in penicillin mould and so place your faith in a tube of pills? Who can guess what is in a little phial or a screw of paper? It could be anything at all. It could be lacking in sympathy. It is therefore for the physicians themselves to help poor, suffering humanity to overcome prejudices and advance with science in great bounds across the Djema'a el-Fna.

Two of the most distinguished of the Marrakeshi street-physicians have accepted this challenge. They have agreed to forget the blows and abuse exchanged when they were competitors and, as Aesculapius said, have joined forces for the common good. One of them brings to the partnership a little yellow powder, the other a dark, viscous fluid in a bottle. There is also a third medicament; a joint prescription, they say. It resembles whelks floating in a clear, golden medium. This is set up in its big bottle, with the whelks crowding the surface of the medium to a depth of several inches. It is expensive and normally only sold in tots, though I dare say princes can afford to buy bottles. In the event of a sale, the liquid is strained off into a tot glass, and the bottle is topped up again from stock.

These two physicians spread out their display on a piece of matting. They have two paraffin-vapour lamps, an advance on the acetylene flares that light most of the others on the *place* after sundown. To the right of the matting are coloured pasteboard charts of the human body, about quarter life-size but quite big enough to show everything clearly. This is not all. It is possible, by opening a succession of little pasteboard windows in the charts, to reveal layers of outlandish organs – lungs and livers and lights, hearts, kidneys and yard upon yard of viscera. The audience is perfectly well aware that these things are to be found in animals and men, but it excites them all the same. It causes the breath to catch in the throat.

Guided slowly through the catacombs of the body by the physician's pointing twig, the mind is softened up for what follows. A stone in the kidney? A breast-pin accidentally swallowed? See what can befall the unwary! And this, says one of the physicians, placing the object in question on the appropriate organ, is what it looks like. Now can everyone understand why this should be so annoying? See how it presses or pricks or rubs against this or that! And worms! Look! There are bottles of them at the other end of the display – awful things, so tenacious and determined. The second physician, who appears to be the senior partner and has hitherto remained disdainfully silent as if he were not really accustomed to sitting on the cobbles with all these goggling peasants standing round him, suddenly adds his deep, bass voice to the attack on ignorance and folly. He reaches for one of the worm bottles.

'These!' he declaims suddenly, shaking the bottle in front of the lamp, 'these were recovered from a noble lady who resides in the Derb Dabashi!'

'The *Lalla Fulaniya*,' interposes the first physician in a whisper. The peasants all nod in shocked agreement. He hands the bottle to one of them so that he can have a closer look. 'Look!'

'Exactly – the *Lalla Fulaniya*.' The senior physician has sat back and is fanning himself. 'And how, you are all asking, were they recovered?'

Everyone glances at his neighbour, wondering, how on earth . . . The senior physician takes a screw of paper from his pocket, bringing it forward to the light, and then – with a sudden flick of the wrist – it lies exposed on his palm. 'With *this*!'

There is a murmur of astonishment. It is the same murmur that further along the *place* follows the storyteller's climax. Quickly the first physician takes his cue. 'How else?' he demands.

'There is no other way known to science. With *this*! This powder!'

'*Lalla Fulaniya* swallowed this powder, and now . . . here . . . in this bottle . . . ' The bottle is agitated briskly, 'and *here* . . . '

'HERE THEY ARE!'

The tempo is getting faster and faster. The physicians can barely pause for breath.

'No griping . . . '

'No pains . . . '

'And all at the most trifling . . . '

'And considering the gravity . . . '

'Insignificant cost!'

'Ten *reál!* Fifty francs!'

'Fifty francs!'

'No more!'

'No less!'

'A single note for ten *reál Marocains*!'

The effect, the timing is brilliant. Hands stretch forward through the welter of *djellabas*, men press closer, the bargaining begins. Science has its foot in the door all right.

* * *

It was extraordinary enough that Fatima should draw, yet still more extraordinary that anyone should be prepared to buy what she drew, but through the kindness and skill of a room-boy at the Hotel Mamounia, a rich, simple tourist has in fact bought one – for five thousand francs! I hurried to the house to tell Fatima this, but she remained quite calm. I don't think she easily visualizes a sum of money so big, and as the payment is by cheque, there are no notes yet to spread out in demonstration. Incidentally, I forgot to say that the picture is of a man bathing in a stream. Fatima says it is a stream called *el-oued l-hamar* which flows near her village. For this reason she has painted it red – the Red Stream. The anatomy of the man is peculiar, and not only because it was drawn in the kitchen without a model. It must be part of Fatima's lyrical vision.

* * *

We have cashed Fatima's cheque and I am sorry to say that directly she saw how much money there was, away went all her good intentions. She snatched the lot and stuffed it into a sort of pocket she has under her apron. I tried to snatch the money back, because the Mamounia room-boy's commission has to be paid out of it, but she said that he had undoubtedly robbed her anyway. I reasoned with her and tried to get at the money again, and she threatened to scream and say I had tried to rape her. As a matter of fact, she did scream and we had a very nasty scene, there on our patio.

Fatima is leaving but I have had the last word. I have told her that just as I invented her, and the Mamounia houseboy made the sale, we have only to un-invent her and she will be done for. I said I would tell the rich, simple tourist who bought it that *I* did the drawing and then he will demand his money back. She doesn't believe me.

*   *   *

Maurice, in the kindness of his heart, has offered me the minute half-finished cottage at the bottom of his orchard. He says that only one of the two rooms will be ready for occupation before Christmas but that he will fix it up adequately. There will, however, be neither light nor water. 'You will be obliged to visit the pavilion for your *toilette*,' he said. 'Do you mind?'

Do I mind? I am enchanted. Anything would be enchanting that enabled me to stay on in Marrakesh, and the room in the wall is an enchantment in itself: minute, a bed, a chest, a chair and a hurricane-lamp. He showed me the shower and the washbasin in the pavilion. The washbasin had become blocked, so we stood talking there while he prodded at the plug-hole with a wire which seems to be kept handy just for this purpose.

'Why do washbasins here – and in France too, for that matter – get so desperately clogged?' I asked him.

'Oh, you English!' he replied. 'And yet we admire you. Your iron discipline, of course. It is that you never put into the lavabo things that are unsuitable for it – whereas we . . . *Regardez!* It is clear again now – *plus ou moins.* I really prefer the Chinese fashion – a big *jarre*, a little pot to dip into it, and water that flows away through a hole in the wall into the garden . . .'

*   *   *

The novel is finished now – not only finished but dispatched and irrevocable. It is a great relief and not less so because I am not very pleased with it. The time approaches for me to move out of Riad ez-Zitoun. Fatima left me ten days ago, and I haven't seen her since. I am sad that we should have parted on baddish terms and for so infantile a reason. I have written to Cato – the friend who was to have been my house-guest and is to visit Marrakesh all the same. I have fixed him up in the Hotel Mamounia for the two days he will be able to spend here. He has written in reply, telling me to expect him on such-and-such a date in January by the midday train from Casablanca – the very train that I came on myself that morning in spring. I wonder what he will think of Marrakesh.

5

El-Minzah

I SHALL CALL IT *el-Minzah* though this should really refer to the pavilion with the panoramic view from its upper stories. From my cottage at the end of the orchard I get no view, except of a twisted vine that grows in front of my door. If I walk out into the orchard I can see the minaret of the Koutoubia towering above me.

Life is very peaceful. If I were asked how I pass my days I should be hard put to it to account for so many long, unmoving hours. Maurice is the perfect host. We leave each other alone, meeting as if by accident. His major-domo brings me my *petit déjeuner* – coffee, rolls and *confiture*. The other meals I take out somewhere. I have visited Madame T. to thank her for all her kindness and she in return pretended, delightfully, that it was she who must thank me for having kept guard over her house all this time. Christmas has come and gone, and in this antique world sunshine and sand seem unexpectedly righter than snow.

Mademoiselle de V. was round at the pavilion today. She and Maurice and I chatted together for a while, and then the time came for her to return home for supper.

'*Tenez!*' she exclaimed suddenly. 'Very nearly I forgot.' She had taken a little packet out of her bag and was holding it out to Maurice.

'*Qu'est-ce que c'est que ça, donc?*' Maurice unwrapped it. It was a painted porcelain doorknob about the size of an apricot. His eyes shone with pleasure. '*Mais, mademoiselle . . . !*'

'I wish you to have it, now that there is no longer need for it *chez nous*.' Mademoiselle de V. closed her bag again and I could not see the expression on her face.

'*Mais . . . non, mademoiselle, non*. You are infinitely kind, but I cannot accept it.'

'*J'insiste*.'

'How is it that you no longer have need of the button, mademoiselle?' I asked her.

'Because *la bressane et la dinde sont . . .*' She hesitated, then looked me straight in the face and added: 'They are eaten.'

'Not by . . . ?'

'No. By me.'

Maurice said: 'I am very grateful – I will mount it upon a *secrétaire* that I am arranging.'

* * *

I was at the station to meet the midday train today but Cato was not on it. *Nīmero six*, the porter who had carried my suitcase for me the last time I was on this platform, saw and recognized me. '*Tiens! C'est l'Américain!*'

I laughed and said that I wasn't American at all but that I probably was the person he thought he knew. Then he said that directly all the passengers had gone – there was the usual breathtaking rush for the exit – we should go together to a *bistro* and drink an *anisette*. I tried to say no but failed under his determination, so we had our drink and then he insisted that we eat together at a little stall a Moor had set up near the station. The next possible train was not due till evening, so I had plenty of time to spare.

After lunch I left *nīmero six* and, rather despondently, went back to the city calling in at the Mamounia in case the hotel had news of Cato. They had. In fact he had already arrived by air. He had left a message for me: he had gone to Maurice's pavilion and would be waiting for me there, if I were not in.

So it did not surprise me to find an empty *taxi-baby* waiting outside our walls. I questioned the driver. He said, yes, it was an English milord, like a Pasha: 'He holds his stick in *this* manner, his head held *thus*, his lips smiling and saying *salām 'aleykum* to the people.' He was evidently very impressed by Cato.

A *taxi-baby* is a very small three-wheeled taxi, powered by a motorcycle engine, with a toadstool for the driver to sit on and a minute double seat behind. *Taxi-babies* stop at nothing and go anywhere where a mule can. I hurried to the pavilion but Maurice's major-domo stopped me on the way. '*Ta camarade est dans la chambre*,' he said, so I turned down towards the cottage instead. Cato was sitting on the bed with the typescript of my novel on his knees and another folder beside him.

'Cato!'

'Well, well, well! I came by air. I hate flying! Dull and dangerous! Didn't you get my telegram? Haven't you been to the telegraph office? I suppose you wonder how I found your house – well, I simply asked at the Mamounia for *Monsieur le Chinois* and they told me at once. I've been here hours – *hours*. Anyhow, never mind. I've got *taxi-baby* waiting – isn't it nice? – and I thought I'd take you out for some culture while the daylight still lasts – I've read it all up – *Guide Bleu*, *Michelin*, a man called Major Something, Budgett Meakin, Augustin Bernard, Edith Wharton, a Frenchman who came in a caravan, Walter Harris – all of them. Culture seems to be very easy here and of course you haven't seen a thing, have you? All this time and not a thing! However, no matter. I shall have the pleasure of telling you all about it. How are you? You look well. I like your cottage – *and* the pavilion – I've seen everything – an Arab as big and noble as a horse showed me round and I caught sight of *Monsieur le Chinois* but he hid himself away and quite right too. Why should he wish to meet me? Now tell me your news quickly, because we really ought to be going. Or you could tell me as we drive along in *taxi-baby*. I very much like driving in *taxi-baby* – did you notice that I had made it take its hood down? And we'll talk about *these*' – he patted the two typescripts – 'later. Very interesting.'

I said: 'I didn't want you to read those.'

'And why not? The novel's for publication, isn't it?'

'Well, I hope so . . . '

' . . . and the other thing?'

'It's just a journal – a personal journal.'

He looked at me in surprise. 'Not read them? And what do you expect me to do, sitting here all this time with nothing but a guidebook I already know by heart? Would you like to examine me on it – the guidebook, I mean? Your novel too, if you like. I've read most of it – and I've just skimmed through the journal.'

I looked unhappily at the novel. Whatever else could be said about it, I knew that it could not please Cato. 'Did you like it?'

'Most interesting,' he said firmly. 'Let's talk about the novel first. I wouldn't change a word of chapter whatever-it-is – the one about that poor camel. Not a single word. But do you know what I'd do in your place – by the way, have you sent it to a publisher yet? You have? Well, I'd withdraw it and I'd sit back and start again from the beginning. Don't refer to this first draft at all, don't look as it (except that camel chapter). Treat it like half-remembered material, dreams, for instance. And another thing – quite a small point but not without importance. Wouldn't you prefer to leave out all the "he saids" and "she saids" and "said hes" and so on? It's a little heavy, isn't it? If you manage it properly, the reader will know at once who's speaking and his eye will be less worried. Do you agree?'

'Excellent idea,' I said. 'Let's put it away, shall we, and go out for some culture? *And* the other thing,' I took the journal from his as well, but he reached for it again.

'While I remember,' said Cato, flicking over the pages of the journal. 'Yes, of course. The journal. Hm–m. Full of . . . do you know, Peter, I don't find a single word about the French? I suggest you infuse them into the text from the beginning. However, that's easily done.'

'I don't see why – '

'Good Heavens! Weren't you planning to?'

'I don't think so. This isn't a journalist's journal.'

'But the French are the most important thing that has happened to

Morocco since the seventeenth century!'

'Of course, but – '

'Well, then?'

I tried to explain. 'Naturally France is important here. She's like the engine of a car. You go driving and you take the engine for granted. You only start thinking about it if it works badly, plugs missing and big ends going and so on. But the mechanics of my life here go so smoothly that I'm not even conscious that it's a French Protectorate, except to be thankful to France for having pacified the country and made it possible for me to live here at all. I don't come into contact with the administrators or . . . '

'Or Moroccan nationalists?' Cato interrupted.

'I don't think I know any – of the sort you mean. Though I suppose everyone, no matter what his country, is a nationalist by instinct.'

'Hm–m,' Cato said, 'I still can't see how you can pretend to live quite untouched by politics.'

'Well, if you insist, I dare say the Pasha's police can be dragged in under the heading – and the municipal refuse-men; I just live a backstreet life here, and the backstreet horizon isn't as far off as a State, or even a district, frontier. Our horizon's the city ramparts and perhaps just far enough beyond them to sniff the air. Of course nationalism is important, but I've been through other people's nationalism before – years ago, in India; and let's face it, nationalists are apt to be bores. As private individuals, I mean. It's like other people in love. *Bores.* I can quite understand the need for freedom, or the need for love as far as that goes, and I want to be free myself – I feel that I am free, and I'm in love with this place – boringly, no doubt. But you know, in spite of the newspapers the great majority of the Moors worry more about living than about concepts of government.'

'Of course you're right. Let's go! *Taxi-baby's* waiting.'

We went. The Koutoubia, the Mosque of Yacoub el-Mansour, the tombs of the Sa'adian sultans, the Minara, the Thursday Market outside the Thursday Gate (the *Bab el-Khemis*), discreet glimpses of the shrines of Sidi bel Abbès and Sidi ben Sliman, the Bahia, the Medersa Ben

Youssef, Dar Si Said, El-Bedi, and finally a breathless circuit of the ramparts in *taxi-baby*, finishing up at the Aguedal. Cato was enchanted.

'Wonderful, wonderful! And you mean to admit it is *I* who must tell you all about these wonderful places?'

What could I say? They are part of the background that influences the people of Marrakesh who in turn influence me, and I am happy to be here surrounded by this magical past that is really the present too. There was no need to say anything, however, because Cato was talking again.

'But the Moors went wrong in the seventeenth century, didn't they – here in Marrakesh in any case? Look at the Sa'adian tombs the guide-books get so excited about! Marble, stucco worked as if it were filigree, over-decorated columns . . . That sort of thing was so much better done elsewhere, in India, Italy. Here it is like it would inevitably be if some Victorian craftsman had re-invented the style. It seems to me that luxury and airy grace are foreign to the Moroccan genius. The Moors need simplicity, space and bigness to show their quality. Look at the ruins of El-Bedi! The same period too. But when it was built and before Moulay Ismail destroyed it out of spite and took away all the marble and chiselled ornament, it was probably just like the Sa'adian tombs but on a bigger scale. Now, with nothing left but the ground plan and crumbling masonry, you can see what I mean about the Moroccan genius for using space as an architectural element.'

I agreed wholeheartedly. I dislike the Sa'adian tombs which beside the Diwan-i-Khas in the old fort of Delhi would seem like store suits beside a Paris couturier's models. Cato hadn't finished.

'Look at the Koutoubia! Look at the mosque and minaret of Yacoub el-Mansour! Both twelfth century and both monuments to the Almohad dynasty. There's the sort of splendour that reflects the true spirit of the Moors! From what I have heard, Moulay Ismail recaptured it in Meknès in the seventeenth century, but with a new emphasis.'

The minaret of Yacoub el-Mansour. It is the minaret I had seen and coupled with the beauty of the Koutoubia the first day I came here. It was nice to have one's purely instinctive judgement supported by a specialist.

'Do you know how it began?' Cato demanded.

'What?'

'Marrakesh, of course. Don't trouble to say "yes", because I propose to tell you. They were men of the Sahara, veiled like Touaregs, and they came raging over the High Atlas some time in the middle of the eleventh century. No sooner had they reached the plains of the Haouz than their leader, Abu Bakr, found himself obliged to hurry off to Mauretania to put down a revolt, leaving his wife and his army in the charge of his second-in-command, Yussuf bin Tashfin. That was the end of poor Abu Bakr, of course. By the time he got back Yussuf had made such progress with the army and with Abu Bakr's wife, and with the invention of Marrakesh for that matter, that he declined to hand over any one of the three. Yussuf was the big shot, now. He had started on a city, and he had dug water conduits, and planted palm groves – to remind him of the oases in his own home-desert, I expect – and here all around us are the descendants of the trees he must have planted! That was the beginning of the Almoravid dynasty. Within forty years the Almoravids were ruling an empire that stretched from Algeria to Senegal. But in less than a hundred years, by the mid-twelfth century, that is, the Almoravids were kicked out by the Almohads. The Almohads are really my favourites: Yacoub el-Mansour was one. Yacoub the Victorious. Even you must know that he built the Giralda in Seville, as well as the Koutoubia here. Then he started on the Tower of Hassan, at Rabat. The Tower of Hassan. Hm–m, well. Yacoub had chosen Rabat as his capital city instead of Marrakesh and of course he wanted to erect a great monument, but . . . The Tower of Hassan – it's a dullish affair, I consider, and only quarter finished because the money and the impulse both ran out, perhaps, and I refuse to call it great merely because it might have been if ever it had been completed and because its builder had done great work elsewhere on the same model. By then the Almohads had had their hundred years and were kicked out in their turn – by new blood they had called in from the Sahara to help bolster up their crumbling authority. So a new dynasty started, the Merinids. The Merinids favoured Fez as their capital, so that Marrakesh was still left out in the cold, and in due course the Merinids crumbled and their place was taken by the Sa'adians. Then the Sa'adians crumbled too. The Sa'adians, I admit, had some feeling for Marrakesh but I have no feeling for them, because of their tombs – but we've already discussed this and agreed about it, haven't we? Then finally the Alaouit dynasty which is still in power, and has been since the seventeenth century. I'm only sorry that that great and wicked Alaouit Sultan, Moulay Ismail, who killed thousands with his own hands and enjoyed it, and was the kind patron of the Corsairs because they brought him Christian slaves from amongst the crews of the British and French and Spanish vessels they were so clever at capturing, who made these slaves build Meknès for him and who wished to marry Louis XIV's daughter by Mademoiselle de Lavallière, the Princess of Conti, but Le Roi Soleil said "no" – you look as if you'd lost the track, Peter. I was about to say that it's a pity the great and wicked Moulay Ismail didn't settle in Marrakesh. Of course he would have destroyed everything that had existed before him – as a matter of fact he did so anyway, except mosques and religious foundations which were necessarily spared, he being a very strict Muslim, but he would have built splendidly again. I look forward to seeing Meknès which he did build. Have you seen it? Anyhow, even if you have not, it would amount to the same thing. Moulay Ismail built palaces like other men build cities, and he bred men like others breed horses and produced a black army of which the descendants form the Sultan's bodyguard today. I don't believe you're listening.'

'Yes. I'm listening attentively.'

Cato smiled. 'It's too late to listen now. I've finished.'

We looked round about us at the palm trees.

'You will dine with me,' Cato ordered, 'and after dinner you will take me to the Djema'a el-Fna. I wish I were staying longer, but I can't. And I want to say one thing more about the "journal". You're being unfair. It isn't Marrakesh you are recording – it's only a tiny interior part of it. You give a completely lopsided view.'

'I live a completely lopsided life, perhaps. But that's the way I live it.'

Cato laughed. 'Then I've no more to say.'

* * *

Cato has gone, leaving me with three guidebooks and a list someone in France had given him of the 'ten people in Marrakesh worth meeting'. None of my friends appears in it. Am I missing something?

* * *

'Aysha came round today, with 'Abdeslem. Apparently she has a very nice American protector now – kind and unexacting. She did not even refer to our little passage of words last time we met: there would be no point in doing so, since she has got what she wanted without my help. I think Moors are quite incapable of harbouring malice. On the contrary, 'Aysha was ecstatically content.

'*Il est tellement riche*, Monsieur Peter! *Ti as vi la nouvelle ceinture de*, 'Abdeslem? *Wurri-h-ha, ya* 'Abdeslem!' 'Abdeslem showed me – a very handsome belt in plaited leather. '*Tivois?*' 'Aysha went on. 'And many other things we have been given.'

'Is your new friend in Marrakesh now?' It was Sunday evening.

'He has returned to his camp. We – me and 'Abdeslem – are now coming back from the cinema. Ah, the beautiful *pellicule!* A Cairo fillum. "*L'Amour Enchanteur*". *Magnifique! Kan meziān b-ez-zāff oula la*' 'Abdeslem?'

'Abdeslem nodded.

'*Ti vois*, Monsieur Peter,' said 'Aysha, laying a shiny new handbag on her knees where I might conveniently admire it; 'you see, these Cairo fillums are most *moderne* of the *moderne*. It is splendid to see! They show how *les messieurs aiment – mais adorent les jeunes filles*, rising from the sofa to assist these beauties into their *manteaux de fourrure*, bringing them rare gifts, beseeching them, crying – *mais oui*, with tears, *avec des larmes véritables* – when the girls do not wish to do as the gentlemen wish. And, moreover, what is it that the gentlemen wish? Do you know? Nothing at all like wish the *cochons* here in Marrakesh – they wish a beautiful thing called Love, Monsieur Peter, and love is to guard these *jeunes filles* from the danger of bandits or monsters, and to give them their heart's desire. And do you know also what is the heart's desire of such modern ladies? I will tell you that too – it is to be protected in this manner, and to be treated sweetly and considered as fine beauties who are not permitted to dirty the hands with common work! Moreover, all these girls can dance and sing and yet are not enclosed in a private and special *quartier*, but free as birds of the air. They resemble, *en effet*, the most feathered of rare birds! The gentlemen in the fillum *worship* them, if I am permitted to use such a word. In short, Monsieur Peter, it is *l'Amour!*'

'What lucky young girls they are!' I exclaimed.

'And more. Do you know, Monsieur Peter, that in America, too, they have *l'Amour?* I know this now. And if you will kindly visit my home next weekend you shall see how it is. And,' she continued vaguely, 'at present my *Americán* friend calls 'Abdeslem my brother – *ti comprends?*'

'I understand. And how do you like this *Amour*, 'Abdeslem?'

'*Ka-idhar-li* – it seems to me – that this *Amour* is pushing the men to where they do not belong.'

'*Ta gueule* – ' 'Aysha commented inelegantly. 'Have you not a new belt, then? No! *L'Amour* is . . . It . . . '

'It makes the world go round, 'Aysha, doesn't it?'

'Exactly!' she cried in triumph. 'Your head is brilliant, Monsieur Peter. 'Abdeslem! Do you hear what Monsieur Peter is saying? *L'Amour* is for making the world go round!'

'A stick is sometimes needed,' 'Abdeslem said, softly and bitterly.

* * *

Tonight Maurice and I were walking as usual on the Djema'a el-Fna. He was saying: 'One chooses – if one can choose – the place in which one shall live for one of two reasons. For me I choose Marrakesh because it is like an extension of myself. With you, Peter, it is different, I think.'

'Go on.'

'For you, Marrakesh represents *le complément* – it provides something that is perhaps lacking in your temperament. Is that so?'

It is perhaps so. I agreed, with reservations.

'In Marrakesh you feel complete, I think. Tell me, you find that Marrakesh enables you to work – *ou le contraire?*'

The contrary is true, of course. I had not thought of it in this way before.

'Particularly with writing, or painting, a man will work in order to complete himself. And if he feels himself to be complete, he will find no need to work. I believe it may be the case with you in Marrakesh, Peter.'

'I think it is the case.'

We had been walking under the moon and when we reached home I said good-night to him in the orchard near the pavilion, and then turned towards my cottage. The moon was sinking and its light lay almost flat across the branches of the fruit trees. It was very dark in the shadows. I switched on my torch and the beam picked out a wolfish dog standing quietly under the vine. It did not move, though I shone the torch on it and we looked at each other for a moment. I said: '*Salām 'aleyk*,' on principle. Then I passed on, only turning to look again when I had reached my door. Still the dog had not moved.

* * *

I was with Idrees the *simsar* and Moulay Yacoub today and happened to mention the dog I saw last night.

Idrees was at once deeply interested. '*Tiens!* You know, *naturellement*, that it is always a cat that is seen in that garden – a cat with her eyes *thus* instead of *thus?*' He made a vertical sign of the with two fingers and then a horizontal one. 'A cat, it is, in that garden, *normalement*.'

I had not noticed how the dog's eyes had been set; they seem round in retrospect, so perhaps they could have been either. Anyway, we were all three much interested. Idrees asked me if I had touched the dog and I said that I had not.

'And a very good thing too,' he remarked with relief. 'If you had touched, then *pfff* . . . '

Quite a lot of people are able to touch dogs without thinking, and though the sort of dogs I saw yesterday are mercifully rare, it is as well that I am not one of those who touch strange animals – so Idrees says. Then Moulay Yacoub told us about a woman white as snow whom he found in his bed some months ago. Her eyes had been set vertically too. He pronounced the formula '*Bismillah er-Rahman ur-Rahim*' at her and she dissolved at once. I am advised to repeat the same formula if I see the dog again. '*Salām 'aleyk*' is not ordinarily enough. But both Idrees and

Moulay Yacoub say they are worried on my account – they hope I will not see the dog-cat again, because even once was too much. It is *not* a good sign.

Then Idrees told us about a devil's changeling that a Berber woman of the Atlas discovered in the basket when she returned from the fields to suckle her newborn baby. There was no need for her to pick it up for her to know that it was a devil's changeling put in place of her two-day-old darling because, no sooner had she crossed the threshold than it flew through the air like a winged thing and attached itself to her breast with its teeth.

'Teeth! At two days! Imagine!' cried Idrees. '*And* a double tongue!'

Moulay Yacoub interrupted at this point to say firmly that of course the woman white as snow found in his bed on the occasion of which he had spoken had had a double tongue too, as one might expect. They wanted to know if we have such things in England and I said, yes, though not often.

Devils get at women sometimes, they say, and then such sprites are born. Moulay Yacoub inclines to believe that Idrees's story of the changeling is more properly the story of a woman who had been got at by a devil. This would be more usual, he says. I had no experience to draw on and made no comment.

There are various kinds of devil: the king of them, Iblis, and then *djinn, 'afreet, shaitan* – others as well, I think, but these are the commonest. The *djinns* – of which the correct plural is *djnoun* and a much blacker, more sinister word than *djinns*, I consider – are born of fire and have human attributes. The Qoran says:

> Shall I inform you upon whom the devils descend? They descend upon every sinful liar, and impart what they have heard, but most of them are liars.

This is taken to refer to the fact that devils are for ever listening at the door of heaven, but, being liars, and in any case not near enough to hear the heavenly conversations at all accurately, the news they impart to their associates on earth is not to be relied upon. It is said that when the angels detect the devils listening at the door of heaven, they come surging out and pelt them with falling stars. The night is full of them.

Moulay Yacoub also said something else – about his house. Even now that he is alone in it (his family having gone to their *bled* to visit relatives), something works the pulley of his well and draws up the bucket. It may be harmless, but the pulley-wheel squeaks and groans, and the sound is dismaying. 'There is no one in the house but me,' cried Moulay Yacoub. 'No one! Not even a dog, or a cat. Not even mice!'

* * *

A Moor I scarcely even know has disturbed me with a chance remark, though the remark itself has importance – 'People say you are not intending to remain here longer . . .'

Who are the people who say this? I haven't even said it to myself because I will not think of it. But it is true, alas. The West still holds me by the leg. I had hoped to be free by now. A year – it is almost a year – should have been long enough, but a tentacle still holds. If I could buy Time, six months more of it, perhaps I could free myself, but there is nothing left to buy it with.

Maurice would feed me. He has told me so, and I pretended to laugh, saying, 'Don't be silly, Maurice.' 'Aysha would feed me too, she says, as long as she has her new 'protector' to pay for everything. 'He is *Americán* of course,' she adds. 'So his feelings are easily hurt. We will therefore not hurt his feelings by telling him, and the days he is here you will not be here perhaps, *yak?*' If only I could learn that gratitude belongs to God and not to men!

The West admonishes me: I am mad to do as I am doing, mad to suspend myself in this eternal, enchanted present. All right, I am mad. And to prove it I have bought an old painted chest, a table, a Berber carpet and a wooden grille for a window. I cannot buy a house, yet I have bought these things to put into it. In defiance, I suppose.

* * *

There is no more to write, now that I have decided. I am going. I have not worked for weeks, though I have made a pretence at it, but there is always something else demanding my attention: a friend, perhaps, or a wish to see the Aguedal now that winter is behind us and the fruit blossom out. On the rough land outside the city the little irises are dead already but asphodel is everywhere and the sun shines for ever in the clean blue sky. I must go before I can think up some reason for changing my mind.

The mechanics of going are so simple. I have merely to buy a ticket while the money for it still remains in my pocket (the return half of my air ticket was long ago sold back to the travel agency). I have only to present myself at the station at the proper time and it will all be out of my hands. I refuse to think what may be going on in my heart.

I have made a round of goodbyes. Idrees, Moulay Yacoub. They spoke to me as if today were like any other day. Haroon – he said, 'Peace on your going . . . Will you return, *Insha' Allah?*' Will I? I made him no answer; poor little Haroon, with difficulties that must accompany him to the grave. Fatima – Fatima all smiles and easy tears and no memory even of our battle in the patio. She had much to say about her present employer, but I didn't want to hear – I cannot bear to think how life will go on in spite of me. She has washed a bundle of my clothes as a farewell present, and I have given her a stud-box. I wonder what she will put in it. It is heartbreaking, this round of goodbyes. The *mul l'hammām*. The *garçons* at the Café de France, busy between parties of new clients and the swabbing of marble tops. One of them wiped his hands on his apron and said, '*Tiens! Ti pars?*' I spoke to those of the regulars who have become my friends, but they wanted to discuss something or other so we discussed it, and in the end I never even told them I was leaving. Then 'Aysha, and 'Abdeslem, with solemn faces as if they loved me. 'There is fog in London, *yak*?' 'Aysha asked. Her fingers were on a woollen scarf that 'Abdeslem had thrown down. Perhaps she was toying with the idea of giving it to me, but if so, she thought better of it. 'Put on your *manteau* always,' she said solicitously, 'and pass my *bonjour* to your dear mother, *n'est-ce pas?*' 'And my *bonjour* too,' 'Abdeslem added, because he is not to be outdone. The night-watchman in Derb esh-Shems. He told me that he wished me to give him aspirin against some improbable malady, but I had none and he said, 'There is no harm in it', so that I should not be upset at having failed him. Moulay Ibrahim and his friend from Derb el-Bir. It is long since I have visited them and they have asked me to deliver a message which is much more like an ultimatum than a message to Seigneur Hamed in Tangier. I did not trouble to say that I was not intending to go by way of Tangier. I tried to find Miriam but she was missing from her hole in the wall, and the Pfaff had gone too. When I visited her mother in their house in the Mellah, Madame Z. said, 'Miriam will be a bride soon, for I have sent her to my sister in Casablanca who is acquainted with an excellent husband. Monsieur Z. and I will go shortly to Casablanca for the inspection. God knows best and will arrange matters in the proper way for Miriam – and no doubt for you too, monsieur.' I saw Bou Djem'a in the café he patronizes but he did not seem to recognize me, nor remember our broken lunch engagement, nor any of our meetings. Because of hashshish, I suppose.

All these lovable, good people who would be surprised at being called anything of the sort. They, who have never gone away – how should they know what parting means, that it means dying a little?

Mlle de V., splendid as ever in her private way. She said 'Why did you not tell me before? I wished to invite you to take a glass of wine with us.'

'I have only just decided. But will you not take a glass of wine with *me*? Now. It is rather a special occasion.'

She paused, smiled serenely, and said, '*Volontiers*, monsieur. Since the occasion is special.'

Maurice. He said: '*La chambre d'ami* will be ready for your return. I will look after your furniture. It is like a gage, the wooden chest and the grille for the window. Will you please remember to send the major-domo a postcard? He very much likes postcards. Every day he searches amongst my *courier* for something for him, but there is nothing.'

'I will write him a letter, then.'

'A postcard is better. It can be shown to everyone, even those who cannot read. Of course it is best if it has a foreign stamp, and if the picture is of a foreign city or of soldiers. Coloured, naturally.'

'Very well. I will do so.'

'And think of us sometimes. I will not accompany you to the station.'

About the Author

Peter Mayne was born in England in 1908. His father was an exotic sort of school master who specialised in the sons of the ruling princes of India and was principal of the Rajmukar College for twenty years. Later he would serve as guardian to the young Maharajah of Jaipur. When Peter Mayne had finished his education in England, he went out to Bombay at the age of twenty and worked as an assistant in a firm of merchant-shippers. He was a failure as a businessman, though his father's many friendships with his ex-pupils permitted Peter easy access to Indian society. At the time of the partition of the Indian Empire he was in Kashmir, and the new Pakistan Government invited him to serve as Deputy Secretary to the Ministry of Refugees and Rehabilitation. After two years had passed, and the tension had eased, he resigned from Government service and moved to Morocco to write.

The novel he wrote in this period was destroyed, though his journal from this period won great critical acclaim and was translated into many European languages. First published by John Murray as *The Alleys of Marrakech* it was reissued by Eland in 1982 under its American title, A *Year in Marrakesh.* Peter Mayne later moved to Athens where he wrote *The Narrow Smile, The Saints of Sind, The Private Sea* and *Friends in High Places* (1975). The latter was a very personal account of an extended visit to Jagut and Mussoorie, two old friends from his youth in Bombay.
Peter Mayne was one of four children. He died in 1979.

ELAND

61 Exmouth Market, London EC1R 4QL
Tel: 020 7833 0762 Fax: 020 7833 4434
Email: info@travelbooks.co.uk

Eland was started in 1982 to revive great travel books that had fallen out of print. Although the list has diversified into biography and fiction, it is united by a quest to define the spirit of place. These are books for travellers, and for readers who aspire to explore the world but who are also content to travel in their own minds. Eland books open out our understanding of other cultures, interpret the unknown and reveal different environments as well as celebrating the humour and occasional horrors of travel.

All our books are printed on fine, pliable, cream-coloured paper. Most are still gathered in sections by our printer and sewn as well as glued, almost unheard of for a paperback book these days. This gives larger margins in the gutter, as well as making the books stronger.

We take immense trouble to select only the most readable books and therefore many readers collect the entire series. If you haven't liked an Eland title, please send it back to us saying why you disliked it and we will refund the purchase price.

Extracts from each and every one of our books can be read on our website, at www.travelbooks.co.uk. If you would like a free copy of our catalogue, please contact us by phone, email or in writing.